Gods and Myths of Ancient Egypt

Egypt

Gods and Myths of Ancient

Mary Barnett
Photography by Michael Dixon

Grange BOOKS

Published in 1999 by

Grange Books
an imprint of Grange Books PLC
The Grange
Units 1-6
Kingsnorth Industrial Estate
Hoo, Nr. Rochester
Kent
ME3 9ND

Copyright © Regency House Publishing Ltd

ISBN 1 84013 352 X

Printed in Singapore

Page 2: The head of Hathor, a capital in the chapel of Hathor in the Temple of Hatshepsut, Luxor.

Page 3: Ani before the gods of the underworld: detail from the Papyrus of Ani, Theban Book of the Dead, c.1250 BC.

Above: Limestone hieroglyphs from an Egyptian tomb of high official Hor-em-heb, c.1350.

Jacket: The goddess Maat wearing the Feather of Truth. 19th Dynasty:1500-1200 BC. Inset left: Papyrus of Hunefer. Anubis: ceremony of Opening the Mouth. Centre: Papyrus of Hunefer: the cat of Ra kills the snake of evil: Apophis. Right: (Luxor Museum) Pharoah Amenhotep III, close-up of face. Back cover: Shu (god of air) supports the boat of Khepri (scarab-beetle creator-god).

CONTENTS

INTRODUCTION

Most people coming into contact with the remains of the ancient Egyptian civilization – through books, films, visits to museums or to Egypt itself – find a colourful and fascinating array of evidence which at first is confusing and largely unintelligible. It is possible to wander among the monuments, the mummies and the hieroglyphs in a museum admiring one thing, wondering at another, but finding it difficult to understand what we see, except in the most simple way.

The experience of everyday modern life hardly equips us to find a common ground with such an alien past, even though much of that past has been so well preserved. The dry climate of Egypt, which slows the processes of decay, and the culture of ancient Egypt, which produced so much in durable material like stone, and preserved so much by elaborate burial practices, have combined to conserve an impressive array of evidence, which is now available for study but remains difficult to comprehend.

To understand the myths and religion of a foreign culture is not easy either, particularly when the culture is as distant in time as that of the ancient Egyptian civilization. The Egyptians used symbols to express abstract ideas, often producing conflicting and contradictory images to express different aspects of the same thing. This book aims to describe some of the elements that formed their myths and helped to give expression to their religious ideas, and to illustrate some of the ways in which those ideas were symbolically represented, particularly in visual terms.

The myths and religion of a country or culture are normally concerned, in their early development at least, with ideas about creation and existence itself, about the relationship of humans with the cosmos and about social order: the ideas that bind and stabilize society, that explain annual and daily events like the recurrence of the seasons and the rising and setting of the sun, and that deal with good and evil, and with dangers and fears, real and imagined.

For the Egyptians the state religion, once established, was concerned with the maintenance of divine order through the king's intercession with the gods; if the gods were propitiated and the king's duties to them were properly performed the state would prosper. This divine order was known as *maat*, meaning truth, order, and harmony. Ritual and magical means as well as practical methods were used to establish and maintain the harmony of *maat* in the state.

For the individual, who was excluded from much of the ritual of the state religion, the concept of *maat* was also important. Ritual, magical and practical means were also used to bring success, to maintain order and to avert misfortune. Household and family gods were probably more important at a personal and everyday level than were the great exclusive state cults. At a personal level too, ethical concepts were evolved which could help an individual to achieve a righteous and worthy life in the present and to attain a pleasant and everlasting afterlife in the future.

One of the difficulties experienced in studying

ancient Egyptian mythology and religion is that images are used symbolically to illustrate a number of different aspects of the same thing. This results in an array of apparently conflicting images. For instance, the sun-god can be illustrated as the sun itself, or as a falcon, or as a human being. What is being worshipped is not the sun, the falcon, or the human image, but the abstract power and qualities that these symbols represent. In this sense the images are not contradictory but are compatible. This book aims to show how some of these symbolic ideas are represented visually, in order to help the reader to understand the concepts they express.

Yet understanding can take us only so far. It is important to remember that Amun, the great god of ancient Egypt, is known as 'the hidden one' and the real name of Ra, the all-powerful sun-god of Egypt, is secret. If Ra's real name were known, his power would be diminished. Amun must always remain the hidden one, otherwise something of his divine mystery and power would also be lost.

A relief from the Temple of Rameses III on the West Bank, Luxor (ancient Thebes) showing prisoners of the campaigns of Rameses against the Sea Peoples.

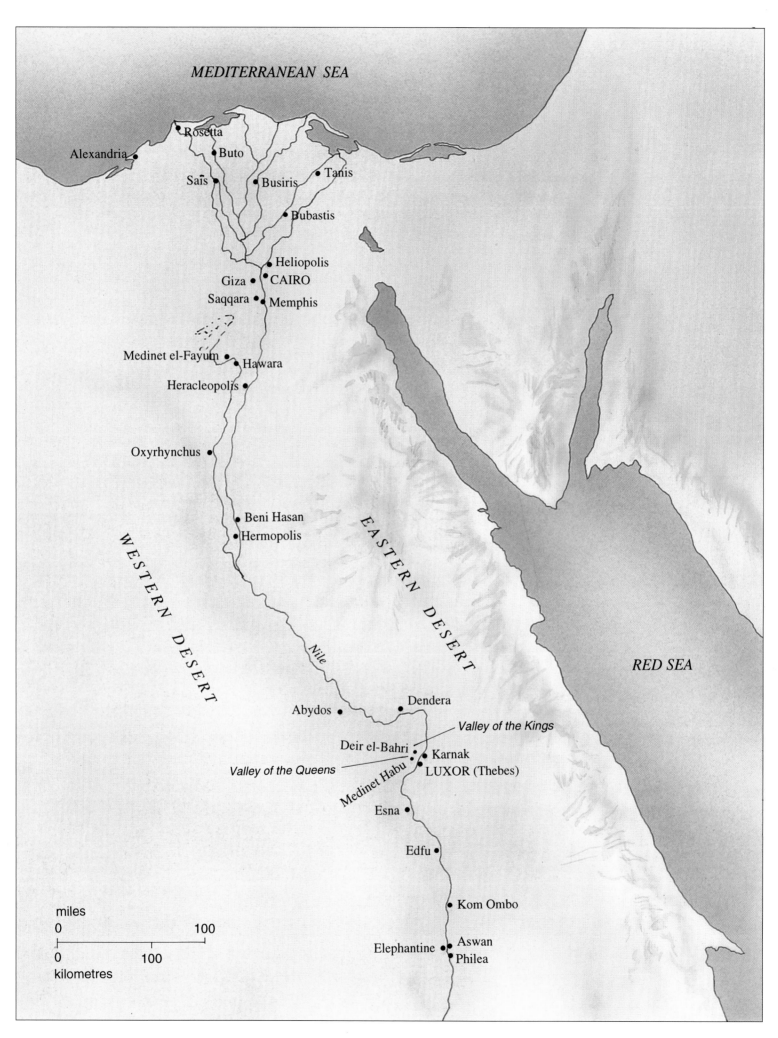

MEDITERRANEAN SEA

Rosetta
Alexandria
Buto
Saïs
Busiris
Tanis
Bubastis
Heliopolis
Giza
CAIRO
Saqqara
Memphis
Medinet el-Fayum
Hawara
Heracleopolis
Oxyrhynchus
Beni Hasan
Hermopolis

WESTERN DESERT
EASTERN DESERT

Nile

RED SEA

Dendera
Abydos
Valley of the Kings
Deir el-Bahri
Karnak
Valley of the Queens
LUXOR (Thebes)
Medinet Habu
Esna
Edfu
Kom Ombo
Aswan
Elephantine
Philea

miles
0   100
0   100
kilometres

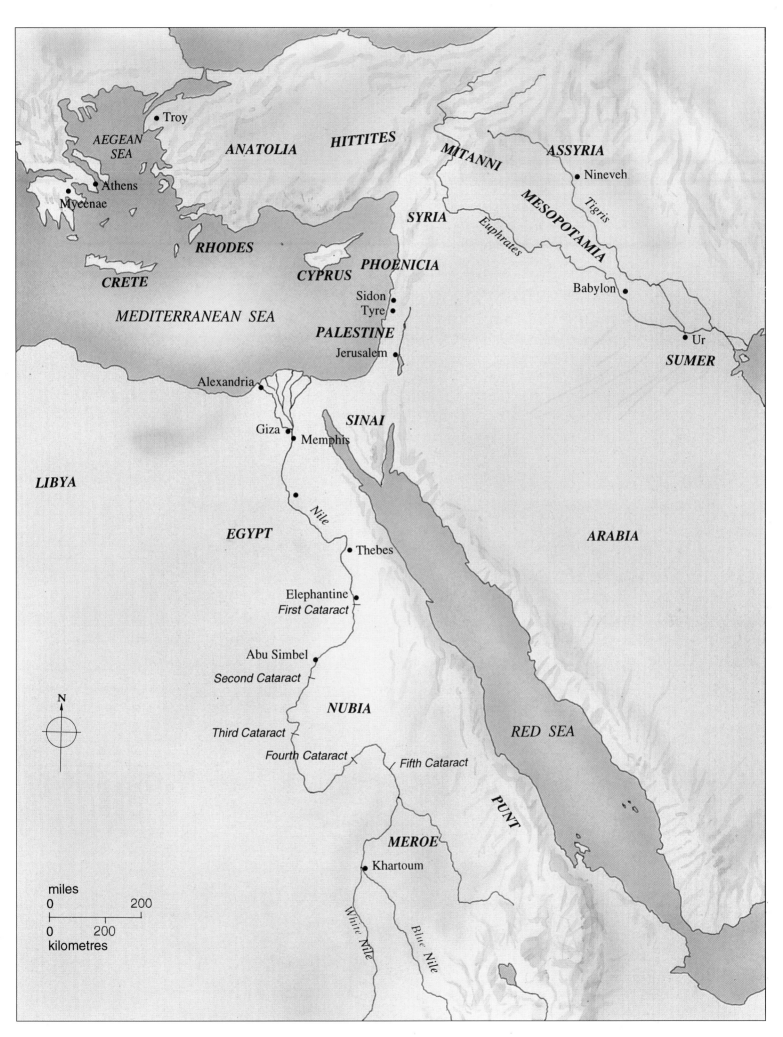

Troy

AEGEAN
SEA

ANATOLIA   HITTITES

MITANNI   ASSYRIA

Nineveh

Athens

Mycenae

MESOPOTAMIA

Tigris

SYRIA

Euphrates

RHODES

PHOENICIA

CYPRUS

Babylon

CRETE

Sidon

Tyre

MEDITERRANEAN SEA

Ur

PALESTINE

SUMER

Jerusalem

Alexandria

SINAI

Giza

Memphis

LIBYA

EGYPT

Nile

ARABIA

Thebes

Elephantine
First Cataract

N

Abu Simbel

Second Cataract

NUBIA

RED SEA

Third Cataract

Fourth Cataract   Fifth Cataract

PUNT

MEROE

Khartoum

miles
0   200

0   200
kilometres

White Nile

Blue Nile

CHAPTER ONE
ANCIENT EGYPT:
LAND, PEOPLE & HISTORY

A stone hand-axe of the Palaeolithic period.

The nature of the gods and myths of any culture is to some extent conditioned by the nature of the land in which the first tellers of their stories lived. The characteristics of the gods and the myths that support their cults and explain their influence change over time as physical, historical and even political events modify the culture that has engendered them. The gods and myths of Egypt have certain features in common with those of many other cultures, but there were also special factors about the geography of Egypt and the development of a strong kingship and priesthood there that have fashioned the myths in a particular way. It seems wise therefore to begin with a general survey of the geographical features of the land of Egypt, and the framework of historical events that influenced the development of its culture.

Egypt lies between the Mediterranean Sea in the north and Sudan in the south and consists mainly of a limestone plateau about 200 to 300m (600 to 1,000 ft) high, which is cut in a south to north direction by the valley of the Nile. On the west the Western, or Libyan, Desert is part of the Sahara Desert, and the mainly limestone rocks are barren and sand-covered. To the east the Eastern, or Arabian, Desert consists of limestone and volcanic rocks forming ranges of low mountains between the Nile Valley and the Red Sea.

The prevailing winds over Egypt are from the north, so that the coastal area receives a moderate rainfall from the Mediterranean and has a Mediterranean climate: but further inland, to the south, the climate becomes that of a subtropical desert. Alexandria on the north coast has about 30 days of rainfall each year, totalling about 180mm (7 in) of rain per annum, while Cairo, about 160km (100 miles) to the south, usually has only about six days rain per year, amounting to about 25mm (1 inch) in total and Luxor hardly sees rain at all, with a rainfall of only about two-thirds that of Cairo.

Without the Nile, most of Egypt would be a barren desert, unable to support any but a tiny nomadic population, and certainly unable to provide a home for a flourishing civilization. But the Nile is one of the world's great rivers, and at about 6,700km (over 4,000 miles) it is one of the longest. Its two main sources are the White Nile, rising from Lake Victoria on the Equator and the Blue Nile, rising in the Ethiopian highlands. The two rivers join at Khartoum, and their waters are later joined by the Atbara from the east.

The White Nile provides a fairly constant supply of water throughout the year, but the Blue Nile and the Atbara are both swollen to a flood by the summer rains in the mountains of Ethiopia. These rains last from late May to early September and in the past, before the building of the Aswan High Dam, they caused the waters of the Nile to rise quickly during June and July and continue rising, more slowly, to reach their maximum level in early September. The waters then subsided quickly during October, and continued to subside more slowly until they reached their lowest point in May when the annual cycle began again.

Over many millennia the Nile carved a channel through the rocks of the Egyptian plateau, making a valley that was only a few miles wide in Upper Egypt but that divided into several channels just north of modern Cairo, and then fanned out into a broad delta before reaching the Mediterranean Sea.

The flood brought large quantities of silt from the Ethiopian mountains, depositing it in the Nile valley where it provided a supply of fertile soil that was renewed annually and that is now over ten metres thick in much of the valley, and up to forty metres thick in parts of the Nile Delta. This régime of annual flooding, which has continued from prehistoric times and throughout the historical period up to the 20th century, has been considerably modified by the building and completion in 1971 of the High Dam at Aswan. This forms Lake Nasser, which stretches southwards as far as the Sudan. As well as

Flint arrowheads from the Sahara, 6th millenium BC.

(British Museum) Detail of the Hunters' Palette from an Egyptian burial of the predynastic period (about 3000 BC) showing hunters with stone axes and clubs, flint knives, spears, bows and hunting dogs.

regulating the floods to provide a more even flow of water in the Nile throughout the year, the dam has meant that much of the silt is held back at the lake, consequently the annual renewal of fertile soil does not now take place.

In palaeolithic times, large areas of Egypt were covered with forests and grassland and the Nile carried huge amounts of water, and silt, from the highlands of Ethiopia, where the rainfall was much greater than it is today. Groups of men hunted game across the whole of North Africa, following a nomadic or semi-nomadic way of life, and settling in the areas that were most favourable to them. Archaeologists have studied evidence of settlements along the plateau overlooking the Nile valley, and have found many flint implements that were used in their hunting and fishing. These settlements and the artefacts were very similar to other Stone-Age settlements in the rest of North Africa and Mediterranean Europe.

There appear to have been movements of people to Egypt from both the east, from Libya, and from the west, from Asia. During the late Palaeolithic period the climate became drier, forest diminished and grasslands gave way to desert. Water and vege-

tation became restricted to a few oases – and to the valley of the Nile. While the surrounding land became more of a desert, the Nile valley became more attractive to the human population.

When the Nile began to rise in late June, the people would move to the higher parts of the valley and during September, when the flood was at its highest, they could hunt gazelle and other animals on the desert plateau. Then in October the water receded, leaving a rich deposit of new mud, and pools and streams full of fish. Wildfowl were also abundant as the Nile provided a natural route for migratory birds. Many plants, including primitive wheat and papyrus, flourished in the rich soil and there was plenty of food. The water level of the river reached its lowest point in the spring so vegetation grew less, but wooded areas in the valley still gave cover for animals that could be hunted for food. When the waters rose again in the following July, the annual cycle was repeated.

Gradually, the population grew and became more settled and became farmers as well as hunters. Those living in the southern part, later known as Upper Egypt, tended more to pastoral activities, while those to the north in the Delta (Lower Egypt)

took advantage of the rich soil and the more temperate climate to become agriculturalists. Simple communities developed along the Nile that were independent of one another for the most part. Archaeology shows that they buried their dead near their dwellings, or in cemeteries on the edge of the desert. They already appeared to believe in an afterlife, for the dead were buried with weapons, tools, jewellery, pottery and food as if it was felt that these things would be needed in the future. The corpse was usually buried in a crouched position, with knees drawn up to the chest, and wrapped in skins or matting. The dry climate often dessicated the body, thus preserving it in a form of mummification that was entirely natural.

Settlements grew in size and labour was organized in the communities to attend to the seasonal work of irrigation, drainage, clearing of channels and building of banks to control and exploit the annual Nile flood for the benefit of agriculture.

A pattern was thus being established that was to develop into the sophisticated structure of the Egyptian civilization. Already there was a natural division of Egypt into two lands, Upper Egypt to the south, and the Delta, or Lower Egypt, to the north.

These areas were to develop into two kingdoms and then they were later to be united to form the one kingdom of Egypt. The capital of Lower Egypt (the Delta region) was Buto; its king wore the red crown; it adopted the bee as its symbol, and the cobra, associated with the goddess Neith, was its chief deity. Similarly, Upper Egypt had its capital at Nekhen, south of Luxor; its king wore the white crown; the sedge was its emblem and its chief deity was the vulture.

The ancient Egyptian period of civilization is traditionally considered to have begun about 3100 BC when Menes, who was possibly the same person as Narmer, united his own kingdom of Upper Egypt with that of Lower Egypt in the Delta. Although the two kingdoms were united by Menes, they kept their separate identities: the king was not 'King of Egypt' but 'King of Upper and Lower Egypt', and the kings of the First Dynasty had two tombs, one near Memphis in Lower Egypt and one near Abydos in Upper Egypt.

Manetho, an Egyptian priest living around 305–285 BC, wrote a history of Egypt and his list of dynasties has been the basis of the modern structuring of Egypt's history. However, the actual order, the

A strain of primitive wheat, similar to that which would have grown in ancient Egypt, growing on an experimental farm at Butser, England.

The Pharoah between two goddesses. The goddess on the left wears the Red Crown of Lower Egypt, the goddess on the right wears the White Crown of Upper Egypt and the Pharoah has the Double Crown of Upper and Lower Egypt. Relief from the outer wall of the Temple of Horus at Edfu, Ptolemaic period.

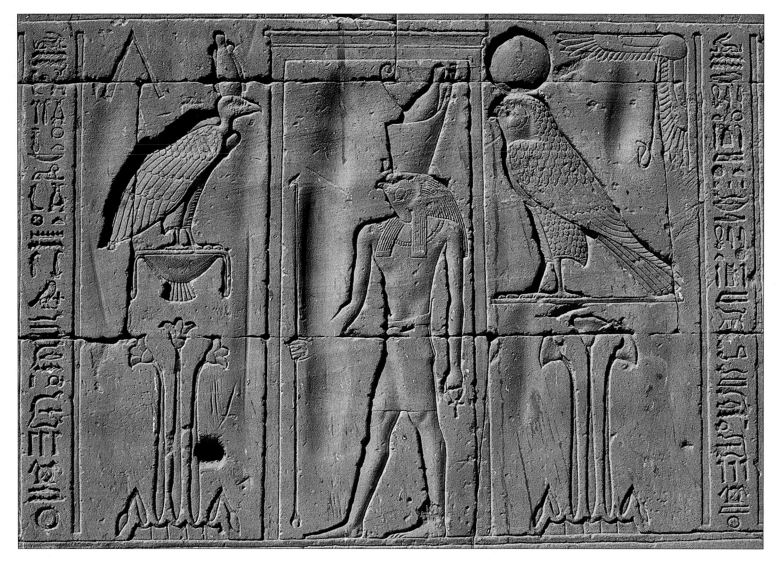

correct names and the exact dates of some of the earlier kings are not precisely known even today. Altogether, there were over 30 dynasties before the conquest of Egypt by Alexander the Great in the 4th century BC, after which Egypt was governed by Macedonian, Greek (the Ptolemies), Roman, Byzantine and Persian rulers before Arab invaders took control in the 7th century AD. The dynasties themselves may be grouped to form several main periods which are summarized here:

EARLY DYNASTIC PERIOD: 1st and 2nd Dynasties: 3100-2686 BC

A new capital was founded at Memphis, south of present-day Cairo, and royal tombs were built at nearby Saqqara and at Abydos much further south. The kings of the 1st Dynasty were buried in *mastaba* tombs, which were formed by digging out a pit in the rock and building a superstructure of mud-brick above it. They were buried with rich tomb furniture, most of which was stolen or destroyed by tomb-robbers, and other burials accompany the main burial, apparently of servants sacrificed at the time of the king's death, to serve him in the afterlife. After the

2nd Dynasty this practice ceased and instead models of servants were buried with the king or other important persons, in the belief that magical spells could bring them back to life to serve their master.

OLD KINGDOM: 3rd to 6th Dynasties: 2686-2181 BC

In this period important buildings began to be built in stone rather than mud-brick, and the first pyramids were built as royal tombs. The most famous 3rd-Dynasty ruler was Djoser (Zozer) for whom the Step Pyramid was built at Saqqara. His chief minister and architect of the Step Pyramid was Imhotep, who was later deified and identified with Asklepios, the Greek god of medicine, becoming a popular domestic deity among the ordinary citizens of Egypt.

Pyramid-building was further developed in the 4th Dynasty, particularly by Sneferu, who built at least three pyramids, including the 'Bent' Pyramid at Dahshur, south of Saqqara, and by his son Khufu who built the Great Pyramid at Giza. Records survive from the 5th and 6th Dynasties of trading expeditions to Nubia, Libya and the nearer parts of Asia. Power became more decentralized, with local courts

Falcon-headed Horus, the mythical king of ancient Egypt, holds the ankh, the symbol of life, in his left hand and the was sceptre in his right and wears the Double Crown of Upper and Lower Egypt. On the left is the vulture of Upper Egypt wearing the White Crown, standing above lotus plants. On the right is the hawk of Lower Egypt, perched above papyrus reeds. Relief from the outer wall of the Temple of Horus at Edfu, Ptolemaic period.

16

and administration in the regions, later called *nomes* by the Greeks. The size of royal tombs decreased, which suggests that royal power and wealth declined then. Worship of the sun-god Ra of Heliopolis increased in importance, and with this the prestige of the priests of Heliopolis increased.

FIRST INTERMEDIATE PERIOD: 7th to 10th Dynasties: c.2181-2055 BC

This was a period of instability, possibly exacerbated by a series of poor harvests, low Nile inundations, and a general decline in central power. Other centres of local power developed as well as the old capital, Memphis. The 9th and 10th Dynasties were centred on Heliopolis, and Thebes became another important centre. Finally a Theban ruler, Mentuhotep II gained control of the whole country, founding the 11th Dynasty and bringing in the next period.

MIDDLE KINGDOM: 11th to 13th Dynasty: c.2055-c.1700 BC

Central power was increased and there was expansion into Nubia. The 12th Dynasty kings ruled from Memphis, and introduced co-regency, whereby the king appointed a successor, usually one of his sons, who ruled with him during the last years of his reign to facilitate a stable transfer of kingship on his death. During the 13th Dynasty, central power declined and the borders of Egypt were subject to invasions by foreigners.

SECOND INTERMEDIATE PERIOD: 14th to 17th Dynasties: c.1700-c.1550 BC

Settlers from Asia established themselves in the eastern Delta and this region, even as far as Memphis, came under the rule of the Hyksos kings, who came from Palestine. The 15th and 16th Dynasties consisted of two contemporary dynasties: Hyksos dynasties ruled in the Delta, while at the same time the 17th-Dynasty Egyptian kings ruled from Thebes. The Hyksos introduced the use of horses and chariots in warfare, and also new forms of weapons, which the Egyptians were later to adopt themselves for their own benefit.

NEW KINGDOM: 18th to 20th Dynasties: c.155-1069 BC

The Theban kings eventually took power from the Hyksos rulers and under Ahmose I, who founded the 18th Dynasty, they gained control of the Delta and of the whole of Egypt. Later, they expanded the Egyptian empire as far as the Euphrates in the east and into the land of Kush in the south. In addition, useful alliances and political marriages were made with other rulers in Western Asia.

Great buildings, especially temples, were built during the period, and the 18th Dynasty included many rulers who are well recorded in the archaeological record and famous still today, for example: Queen Hatshepsut, Amenhotep III, Akhenaten, Tutankhamun, Horemheb. The 19th Dynasty continued with Rameses I and II and Seti I and II among others, and the 20th Dynasty had a succession of Rameses as rulers.

The New Kingdom period, which had started as a period of expansion and of great architectural, artistic and literary achievement, declined by the end of the 20th Dynasty. There were increasing attacks from abroad, notably by the Sea Peoples, and power shifted away from the kings towards the priesthood of Amun.

THIRD INTERMEDIATE PERIOD: 21st to 24th Dynasties: 1069-747 BC

Power was now decentralized. Smendes, the founder of the 21st Dynasty, ruled Northern Egypt from Tanis in the Delta: at the same time the priest-kings of Amun at Thebes (such as Pinudjem I) controlled Southern Egypt. A Libyan, Sheshonq I, gained power in the Delta, founding the 22nd Dynasty, and for a short time he established his son at Thebes. Then Egypt was again divided, with the 22nd, 23rd and 24th Dynasties ruling simultaneously in different parts of the country. The 25th Dynasty, Kushite, expanded northwards from Kush and gained control of Thebes, but could not displace the 24th Dynasty that was still ruling the Delta from Saïs.

LATE DYNASTIC PERIOD: 25th to 30th Dynasties: 747-332 BC

The 25th Dynasty Kushite ruler, Shabaqo, moved his capital northwards from Thebes to Memphis, but a number of Assyrian invasions aided by rulers from the Delta culminated in the overthrow of the Kushite Dynasty and the rule of Egypt by the Assyrians. When the Assyrians withdrew from Egypt because of troubles nearer home, Psamtek I established the Saïte Dynasty, the 26th, as the major power in Egypt. At this time Greek mercenaries were brought into the Egyptian army and Greek traders settled along the Mediterranean coast.

The Greeks and Egyptians had a common enemy – the Persians – and in 525 BC the Persians invaded Egypt and established the 27th Dynasty. In 404 BC the Egyptians shook off Persian rule and during the 28th, 29th and 30th Dynasties Egyptians ruled their own land again until

The Step Pyramid of Djoser stands on the edge of the Western Desert overlooking the Nile flood-plain. The palm trees mark the western edge of the Nile Valley at Saqqara, near Memphis, which was the capital of Egypt at the time of Djoser.

The Pyramids of Khufu, Khafre and Menkaure (from right to left) at Giza. These were the largest pyramids built by the Pharoahs.

the Persians returned under Artaxerxes III and held Egypt from 343 to 332 BC.

MACEDONIAN AND PTOLEMAIC PERIODS: 332–30 BC

In 332 BC, Alexander the Great, having beaten Darius III of Persia at the Battle of Issus in Asia, made a brief diversion from his conquest of the Persian Empire in Western Asia to free Egypt from the Persians. On Alexander's death, Egypt passed briefly to his immediate successors, then to Ptolemy I Soter, who had been the Macedonian administrator of Egypt. The Ptolemies ruled from 305 to 30 BC, establishing a new capital at Alexandria, increasing the influence of the Hellenistic world upon Egypt but also retaining the existing Egyptian religious and

(British Museum) Horse and chariot and attendant. Wallpainting from the tomb of Nebamun at Thebes, c.1400 BC.

political system. They repaired, enlarged and founded new temples and introduced the cult of Serapis which assimilated both Egyptian and Greek religious ideas.

ROMAN PERIOD: 30 BC–AD 337

Egypt played its part in the power struggle between Pompey, Julius Caesar, Mark Antony and Octavian (Augustus) for control of Rome, and Cleopatra VII, her brother and her son Caesarion were to be the last of the Ptolemies. The Roman Emperors succeeded as Pharoahs, but Egypt was seen by the Romans chiefly as a source of food, of exotic goods and of taxes. Some Emperors, notably Hadrian, travelled in Egypt and showed an interest in Egyptian culture and religion.

Cleopatra and her son by Julius Caesar, called Caesarion, making offerings to the gods. Relief on the outer wall of the Temple of Hathor at Dendera. Cleopatra wears the cow's horns holding the sun-disc of Hathor, who was regarded as the divine mother of the reigning Pharoah. She holds a libation vessel and a sistrum. Caesarion wears the double crown and the ram's horns of Amun, and holds out a censer to present incense to the gods. Above him a hawk , symbol of Ra the sun-god or of Horus, stretches out its wings protectively.

In the 4th century AD the Emperor Theodosius ordered that all Egyptians should become Christians and that all pagan temples should be closed. Some areas survived this measure for a while, but in AD 553 the Emperor Justinian finally closed the temples at Philae and Siwah, effectively making an end of the ancient Egyptian religion. A special form of Christianity, Coptic Christianity, had developed in Egypt and its early forms show some assimilation of Egyptian religious elements, and of Greek mythological ideas also.

Egypt became part of the Byzantine Empire, and its borders were raided by North Africans from the west, by Nubians from the south and by Sassanian Persians from the East, until in the 7th century AD a successful invasion established the Arabs and Islamic religion in Egypt.

With the destruction of the Egyptian religion and the scattering of its priesthood, the meaning of hieroglyphic writing was lost until its decipherment in the 19th. century. Consequently there developed a mystery about the Egyptians and their religion which remains to this day.

CHAPTER TWO
UNCOVERING ANCIENT EGYPT

Any real understanding of Ancient Egyptian civilization was dependent upon the decipherment of Egyptian hieroglyphics, which did not come about until the 19th century. Yet Europeans retained an interest in the civilization and, over the intervening centuries, gleaned what they could from visiting the country and observing and collecting its antiquities. Even though the secret of hieroglyphics was lost, other early sources of information about ancient Egypt were available to Europeans.

The most important of these was the description of Egypt by the Greek writer Herodotus in his *Histories,* written about 425 BC. He had visited Egypt in about 450 BC and writes mainly about the Delta, although it seems possible that he travelled as far south as Aswan. He obtained much of his information from Egyptian priests. Nevertheless, he was a close observer at first-hand and describes the country's religious customs, including festivals, the use of magic, animal cults, burial customs and mummification. Although some of his information has proved unreliable, later research has shown that a great deal of it was true.

Another Greek writer, Diodorus of Sicily, visited Egypt in about 60 BC and his World History contains a description of Egypt based partly on material from earlier sources including Herodotus. Interestingly, he added material on mummification not recorded by Herodotus. He also gave a brief account of the Osiris myth, which the writer Plutarch, a Greek citizen of Rome, later described in more detail.

Many travellers visited Egypt during the Roman period. They usually arrived at the port of Alexandria and followed the Nile to Memphis, Giza and Thebes, sometimes travelling as far as Elephantine. Strabo, one of the great, learned travellers of the Roman world, went to Egypt in 25 BC, spent a few years in Alexandria and travelled as far as the First Cataract. The last book of his *Geographia* contains an account of Egypt, particularly of Lower Egypt, that became an important reference work for later travellers. Pliny, Plutarch and Josephus were other writers from the Roman world who added to the early accumulation of knowledge about ancient Egypt.

Later, some of the evidence for the ancient civilization was destroyed during the Christian period in Egypt, in the first millenium AD. Many of the temple reliefs and inscriptions were defaced because Christians regarded them as idolatrous. Parts of some temples were actually converted into Christian churches, while others had houses built within them or were used as convenient quarries to provide stone for local builders.

In fact, few travellers visited Egypt from then until the 16th century, when it became a Turkish province. At that time trade with Europe increased, encouraging more European visitors to Egypt. In the 18th century travel became fashionable among wealthy Europeans, many of whom visited Egypt. An interest in collecting Egyptian antiquities developed among these visitors and created a considerable

Strabo described the Colossi of Memnon (Amenhotep III) at the site of his mortuary temple. The temple stood in the inundation zone of the Nile, and the flooding and robbing of the stone by later kings to build their own temples completely effaced the building, leaving only these two colossal figures of Amenhotep III which stood at the entrance to the temple. The former flood-plain of the Nile can be clearly seen, and beyond this is the steep western edge of the Nile valley. The Valley of the Kings, where many of the New Kingdom kings were buried, lies in these hills behind the colossi. Strabo mentioned that one of the figures emitted a singing sound when the first rays of the morning sun struck it. At first Strabo thought the sound was caused by locals, but became convinced of its supernatural origin. It may have been caused by a flaw in the stone and expansion caused by the sun's heat. The sound ceased when Septimius Severus later repaired the monument.

industry among both the local people and the collectors. Antiquarians from France, England, Germany and Italy acquired collections of Egyptian antiquities that can now be seen in the museums of Paris, London, Berlin and Turin as well as in other cities throughout Europe. Interest in the country was also indicated by the many detailed topographical studies that were published.

When Napoleon Bonaparte invaded Egypt in 1798 he instigated a programme of research into all aspects of Egyptian civilization – scientific, cultural and historical. It was carried out during the period of French occupation and resulted in a 19-volume work: *Description de l'Égypte*, published from 1809–1828.

One of the most significant findings of the French came by chance, however. In 1799, while the French army was working near Rosetta to improve coastal defences against the British, they found a stone that bore three long inscriptions written in three language forms: hieroglyphic, demotic and Greek. This stone passed into British hands after their victory over the French. It now lies in the

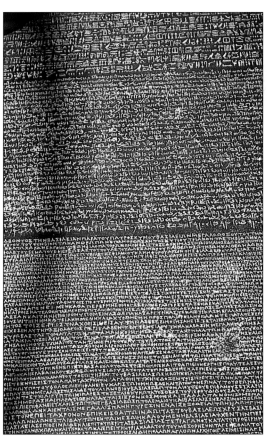

British Museum and is known as the Rosetta Stone. There was no difficulty in translating the Greek text inscribed on it, which proved to be a decree issued by Ptolemy V in 196 BC. Then it was realized that the demotic and hieroglyphic texts were direct translations of the Greek text, and thus the possibility of deciphering hieroglyphs was at last glimpsed.

After a few false starts by various scholars, one Thomas Young realised that hieroglyphs could be used either phonetically, where each hieroglyph stands for a sound, or ideogrammatically, where each hieroglyph stands for an idea related to is pictorial value. By referring to the Coptic language and script, Young was able to decipher the demotic part of the inscription and go a little way towards deciphering the hieroglyphs. A Frenchman, Jean-François Champollion, continued the work and, in 1822, published a description of Egyptian hieroglyphs that at last made the ancient texts, papyri and inscriptions accessible after about 1500 years of obscurity.

Briefly, hieroglyphic script was the original form of writing developed by the Egyptians; it used signs written in lines without punctuation marks or spaces to indicate breaks between words or sentences. The letters 'face' towards the beginning of the line they are in: thus, if the human or animal heads face to the left, the line should be read from left to right, and vice versa. Columns are always read from top to bottom. There are no signs for vowels, only for consonants. This means that the exact pronunciation of ancient Egyptian cannot be known, although some clues have been obtained from the Coptic language, which is a later form of Egyptian written with Greek letters together with a few signs derived from hieroglyphs.

The signs could be used in three ways. First, they could be used as phonograms, with each sign representing a single consonant such as p, or with each sign representing two or three consonants such as pr or nfr. Second, they could be used as logograms, in which a picture sign of an object would actually mean that object. Third, they could be used as determinatives placed at the end of a word made up of phonograms to modify the meaning of the word; for example the letters making up the word

(British Museum) Hieroglyphs on the stela of Inyotef from Abydos. 12th Dynasty, c.1930 BC.

(British Museum) Egyptian hieroglyphs, a list of funerary offerings on the tomb of a state official, c.2550 BC.

for wife may be followed by a sign, the determinative, illustrating a seated woman.

Hieratic script developed about 2700 BC and has simpler forms than the hieroglyphic signs. It allowed faster writing on papyrus, and hieratic script was used chiefly for literary and administrative texts. Demotic script evolved from hieratic script about the 7th century BC and was used in commercial and administrative documents, and later in literary, technical and even religious documents. Its use died out in the second century AD as Roman administrators used Greek for official and legal documents, while the Copts used the Egyptian language written in a Greek script with a few additional signs.

The ability to understand what was written in texts and papyri and on inscriptions on stone obviously encouraged new, more informed, work on the antiquities of Egypt and enabled a far more scholarly approach to be instigated. In 1858 the Egyptians appointed their own Director of Antiquities, and began to control the export of antiquities from the country and to form a national collection, which they eventually housed in its own purpose-built museum, The Egyptian Museum in Cairo. Many other countries have nevertheless continued to excavate, to conserve and to research, so that our understanding of the gods and myths and the civilization of ancient Egypt continues to grow year by year.

CHAPTER THREE
EGYPTIAN RELIGION

(Egyptian Museum, Cairo) The Pharoah stands between Sekhmet (the lion-headed goddess) and Ptah. On the left is the vulture of Upper Egypt wearing the White Crown, balanced on the right by the cobra of Lower Egypt. The king wears the Blue Crown and carries the flail and crook, symbols of royal authority. Pectoral from the tomb of Tutankhamun, 14th century BC.

A first introduction to Egypt's past, through books, museums, or a visit to Egypt itself, leaves a fascinating, colourful, and confused impression. The impression is also a biased one, particularly in the case of myths and religion. One reason it is biased is that most of what has been preserved has come from tombs and burials. Much of our knowledge of everyday life in ancient Egypt is derived from tomb furniture, objects buried in tombs, models placed in tombs, scenes painted in tombs.

They give an impression of a society obsessed with death, or at least with the afterlife. They show evidence of great wealth and luxury when we know that the majority of the population would have been poor, or at least not very rich, and would have left very little behind them for us to see. We, of course, are not able to visit them in their ordinary houses, nor to observe them going about their daily activities.

When we examine their religion we find literally hundreds of gods, many of them animals, or humans with animal heads, some of them monsters unlike any animal we have ever seem. It is not possible to know what the innermost religious thoughts of these ancient Egyptians were. It would have been true then, as it is true today, that at any one time there would be a hundred different people with a hundred different shades of religious feeling, and as times changed, those religious ideas would have changed too.

Myths would also have changed and become

adapted, been created and been forgotten. The Egyptian civilization lasted over three thousand years, a time-scale that would take us back from our present day to a time before the beginnings of Rome and before the flowering of ancient Greece. Words spring to mind to describe the religion we see in ancient Egypt: totemism, fetishism, polytheism, magic – all true in sense. Yet it has been argued that despite all this there is a strong monotheistic tradition in ancient Egyptian religious thought. A reading of the so-called Wisdom Literature and other ethical writings confirm this view and will be discussed later in this book.

Furthermore, our own society is so different from theirs, and our own religious cultural background, whatever our own specific religious beliefs, is again so different that it is impossible to know precisely what was the religious experience of the ancient Egyptians. However, we can study the rituals, the outward forms, the symbolism, the development and evolution of their religion and thereby gain some understanding of its mysteries.

The Nile itself was an important element in ancient Egyptian thought. The black alluvial soil of the Nile valley contrasted with the red rocks of the desert on either side: the Egyptians called them the Black Land and the Red Land. The narrow valley of Upper Egypt contrasted with the Delta region of Lower Egypt. The annual cycle of inundation suggested the concepts of creation, and of death and rebirth. The sun, rising daily above the hills of the east and setting in the deserts to the west suggested another regular cycle of renewal. These natural events tended to provoke similar mythologies among many primitive peoples, but the marked contrast between valley and desert, and the special conditions of the annual Nile flood made a unique impression upon the early inhabitants of Egypt.

The Nile was the main thoroughfare of ancient Egypt, and the boat was the best means of travelling any distance. Consequently, when the ancient Egyptians thought of the sun-god travelling across the sky by day, they imagined that there was a river in the sky along which the sun-god sailed in his solar

The Temple sacred to Amun, Mut and Khons at Luxor. Sphinxes line the processional way which led from the Temple of Amun at Karnak to Luxor, ending at the great pylons of the temple.

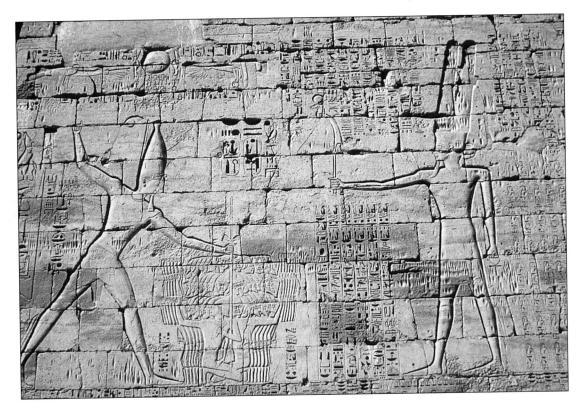

Rameses III smites the enemies of the realm in a public declaration of his power on the outside wall of one of the pylons at the entrance to his temple at Medinet Habu near Luxor.

boat. Similarly, they believed that at night the sun sank below the western horizon and travelled through the underworld, sailing over water in his boat, to emerge next morning at the eastern horizon. At these latitudes the power of the sun could be both beneficial and life-threatening, and the absence of the sun during the dark and cold desert nights was a contrasting feature of the environment. This could be the basis of the thread of dualism which runs through Egyptian thought: day and night, east and west, desert and river, flood and drought, sowing and harvest, death and rebirth, good and evil. These are universal themes of myth, but they were perhaps more intensely felt in the Nile valley than they were elsewhere.

In predynastic times the dead were buried with objects that may have had some kind of religious significance. There were female figures of baked clay and of ivory, small animal figures that might have been worshipped, and slate palettes in the form of animals such as the hippopotamus. Useful everyday objects were also buried with the dead, and these might have been buried with the intention of providing them for use in an afterlife.

Early predynastic Egyptian pottery, particularly from the Delta region, sometimes bears painted designs which resemble the standards displayed on boats or carried by men. The Narmer palette (c.3100 BC) shows a procession of four standard-bearers, each standard surmounted by a bird, mammal or other object. These may be totems, and may be the forerunners of the animal cults that continued throughout the period of Egyptian civilization. The word 'totem' actually comes from North America but is commonly used to express a concept found in Ancient Egypt. It is derived from an Algonquin word meaning the emblem of a tribe or group. The totem usually took the form of an animal (less commonly a plant or other natural object) that identified the tribe or group. The animal itself was often perceived as an ancestor of the group, and seen as a guardian spirit who might be appealed to or worshipped.

The early inhabitants of the Nile valley formed independent groups with their own territories within the Nile valley and, when Egypt was united, the country was divided into regions based on these territories. In Ptolemaic times these regions were called by the Greek word *nomes*. There were about 40 nomes in the whole of Egypt, and each had an insignia, or standard, and could be described as the 'jackal nome' or 'ibis nome' after the animal or other device on its standard. A group probably chose a particular animal because it had certain qualities they respected or feared. A snake, hawk, jackal, scorpion or crocodile are all obvious choices from the local animal population.

Some of the objects on the standards were not animals but other objects, which might have been fetishistic in character. A fetish (the word comes from West Africa) is an object worshipped for its magical powers, acting as a charm or amulet, and revered in its own right rather than as an image or symbol of something else. There are many examples of fetishism, magic, and the use of amulets and spells throughout the history of ancient Egypt, for example the shield and crossed arrows that were a symbol of the warrior-goddess Neith have been found on emblems dating from as far back as predynastic times.

Different regions had their own local gods, and cult centres developed with their own gods and their own mythologies. The chief ones are set out on the chart opposite.

The god of a particular district would be worshipped locally, but would rise to prominence nationally if the rulers of that district became national rulers. Thus Horus, the god of the rulers from Hieraconpolis who unified Egypt at the start of the dynastic period, gained status from their political success. Similarly Amun, who had been an obscure local god, rose to national importance as the god of the Theban kings who drove out the Hyksos from Egypt. Neith, a warrior-goddess from Saïs, became important in the 26th Dynasty when Egypt was ruled by kings from Saïs. Throughout the history of ancient Egypt political events shaped the development of religion while myths were invented or modified to suit political ends, as we shall show.

A profusion of gods existed, and the priests of

MAIN CULT CENTRES IN ANCIENT EGYPT.

Locality:	Local Deity:
Buto	Edjo (cobra goddess), later Horus
Saïs	Neith
Tanis	Seth
Busiris	Osiris
Heliopolis	Atum or Ra
Memphis	Ptah & Sekhmet
Hermopolis	Thoth
Thinis	Onuris
Abydos	A Jackal, later Osiris
Dendera	Hathor
Koptos	Min
Ombos	Seth
Thebes	Amun
Edfu	Horus
Elephantine	Khnum

Seti I offering incense to the god Horus. Wall painting from the sanctury of Horus in the Temple of Abydos.

the cult centres would modify existing traditions to develop complicated mythologies in order to establish the superiority of their own local cult and gods above those of their neighbours and rivals. The practice of the cults became exclusive to the king and the priesthood. Temples were not built for public worship, but for the private practice of the cult by the king and the priests.

The king was seen as the son of Ra, the sun god, and as the living king he was Horus, the mythical king of Egypt and successor of Osiris. When he died, the king was carried to the sky to live with Ra and to take his place among the stars. But with the rise to prominence of the Osiris cult, the dead king was thought of as Osiris, the mythical dead former king, who ruled in the underworld.

The most important duty of the king was to maintain the *maat* of Egypt, *maat* being the state of divine order and justice, and this involved a daily ritual in each temple, before the shrine of the god. The king was meant to perform the ritual in person, but as he obviously could not do this at every temple throughout the land, his place was taken by a priest as his representative. The daily ceremony started as a procession to the temple followed by the ritual purification and dressing of the king in the House of Morning. A censer was charged with charcoal and incense for the king and he proceeded to the shrine of the cult statue of the god. The doors of the shrine were unsealed and opened and the king offered incense to the god and presented the figure of Maat to the god to represent order in his kingdom. The figure of the god was then stripped of its garments, purified and re-clothed in fresh garments.

A ritual feast was prepared on an offering-table in front of the shrine. The courses of food were consecrated and offered to the god, more incense was offered and the doors of the shrine were closed and re-sealed. Then the room which contained the shrine was purified and all footprints were swept away as the king retreated from the room. The public did not attend this ceremony; it was a ritual that involved only the king and senior priests, and like many aspects of the state religion it was remote from the experience of ordinary people.

Only at the great annual festivals, when the gods would be brought out of the temples did the general population participate in the great state cults. In the second month of the inundation, Amun would travel from his temple at Karnak to visit the shrine of his consort, Mut, at Luxor. At another time, Hathor would make the long journey by boat on the Nile from Dendera to celebrate her divine marriage to

Horus in his temple at Edfu. There were pilgrimages and festivals at the shrine of Osiris at Abydos, a festival of the Coming Forth of Min at harvest time, a festival of Sokar near the end of the inundation season. Such festivals were times of holiday for the ordinary people.

The *sed* festival was concerned with the role of kingship rather than with one particular god and was first documented in the reign of king Den in the 1st Dynasty. This festival celebrated the royal jubilee after the king had reigned for 30 years, although in some cases it was celebrated well before the full 30 years had elapsed. There was a double coronation to confirm the king as King of Upper Egypt and of Lower Egypt. As part of this ceremony, the king ran a course between markers, probably to symbolize the boundaries of his kingdom, although the running of the course may have been to demonstrate his physical fitness for the kingship. Then the king fired four arrows, one to each of the four cardinal points, symbolically directed at the enemies of his realm.

The temple was a dwelling-place for the gods

where the king could commune with them and act as an intermediary between them and the people. The inner rooms of the temples were covered with paintings showing the king worshipping and making offerings to the gods. It was believed that these images could take the place of the king in his absence and perform the essential rituals that were required by the gods. The status of the king was reinforced by images on the temple walls that showed him being blessed by the gods, and in the birth-houses attached to the temple the king would be shown symbolically as a child of divine origin.

The king was the First Prophet or High Priest of every temple, but a chief priest was appointed to deputize for him. This person would often be the nomarch, or ruler of the local province of which there were some 40 in Egypt, or some other high local official. Another senior priest would manage the economy of the temple and other priests would attend to specialized duties within the temple, including the study of astronomy, the teaching of writing and the copying of religious texts, singing

(British Museum) Athu a priest of Amun, and his wife who was a priestess. 18th Dynasty, c.1430 BC.

and making music for the temple ceremonies.

The ordinary priests were organized in four groups: each group would serve at the temple for one month and then return to its secular life for the next three months. During its month of office the group was paid from the temple revenues, and the position could be a lucrative one. It was believed that only the essence of the food offerings brought to the gods every day was consumed by them so the priests were free to consume the actual offerings. The priests were thus concerned with the temple and its organi-zation. It seems very unlikely that they performed any kind of pastoral role.

Many temples and priesthoods were granted freedom from taxes and state service and were able to become rich and powerful, at times even rivalling the authority of the king. The consequent rivalry between temple and king is well illustrated by the events of the reign of Akhenaten who reduced the power of the priests of Amun at Thebes and favoured the hitherto less important cult of Aten, retaining exclusive control of that cult to himself. On the death

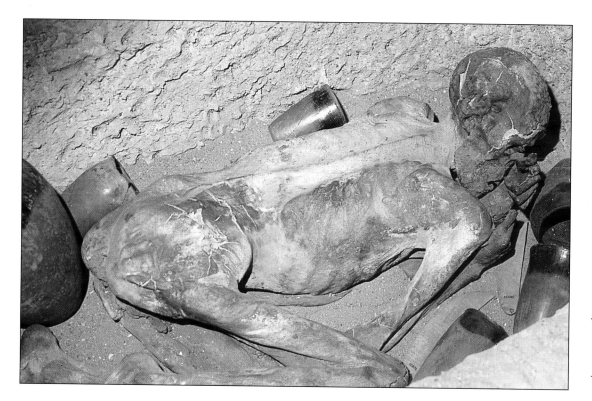

of Akhenaten, the priests of Amun were able to regain their lost power and influence and to efface much of the work of Akhenaten. Temples developed into great administrative centres, and the priests became substantial landowners, employing large non-priestly staffs to run the temple estates.

The records show that Rameses III endowed about one tenth of all cultivable land in Egypt to temples, while the temples also received income from private donations and from tithes. When the temples acquired land they also acquired control of the people who lived on that land so that, although the state religion itself was often remote from the people, the religious institutions actually had a direct influence on the lives of many of them.

The ancient Egyptians held the fundamental belief that life could continue after death in some form or other, but for life to continue in a form similar to that of their present life, the body and the spirit of the individual had to be preserved and the needs of both body and spirit had to be attended to. In addition, to gain an eternal afterlife the person had to show piety to the gods and lead a good and just life in the present world.

The preservation of the physical self was achieved by mummification of the body, and by the encasing of the mummy in a suitable coffin within a tomb that would protect it from decay and destruction. In many simple burials of predynastic times the body was preserved by natural dessication arising from the dry climate and contact with the sterile sand of the burial place. Later, when the dead were buried in more elaborate tombs this natural process of

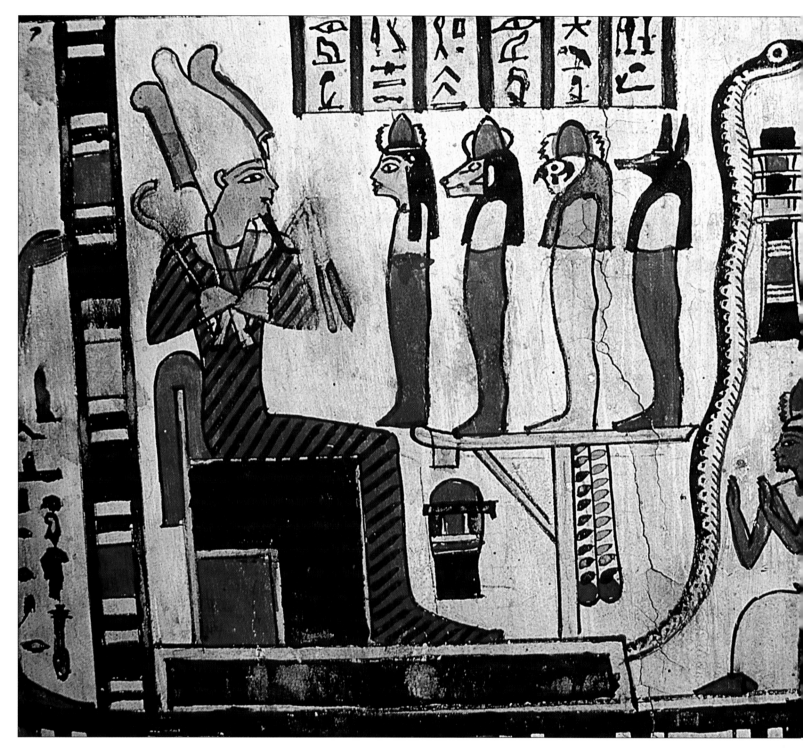

preservation did not take place and putrefaction of the body occurred. In order to preserve the body under these conditions, a process of mummification was evolved, which gradually achieved the desired result.

By the time of the New Kingdom this process was quite advanced. The brain and viscera were removed from the body, as these speeded the process of decay, and they and the body itself were dehydrated by the application of natron, which is a naturally-occurring form of sodium carbonate and sodium bicarbonate found in a number of locations in Egypt, particularly at Wadi Natrun in Lower Egypt. The heart, regarded as the seat of intellect, was usu-

ally left in the body. The body was treated with oils, resins and spices and then packed out to restore its original contours as the dehydration process caused the flesh to shrink and the body to become mainly skin and bone. Amulets were placed on the body as a form of protection, and it was wrapped in linen bandages. This became a very skilled process, which reached its highest standard in the 21st Dynasty but tended to deteriorate thereafter.

The internal organs, which had been taken out earlier, were also carefully preserved because no part of the body should be missing if it was to be perfect in the afterlife. They were stored in four canopic jars, and placed near the mummy at burial. The word

Salt 1821.

canopic, used to describe these jars, arises because their swollen shape and animal-headed stoppers reminded early scholars of the story of Canopus, the pilot of Menelaus, who was buried at Canopus in Egypt, and was worshipped there as a jar with a human head and a swollen body.

The contents of the canopic jars were protected by the four sons of Horus, each assigned to a particular organ. Duamutef, identified by his jackal's head, protected the stomach: Hapi, with the head of an ape, protected the lungs: Imsety, with a human head, guarded the liver and Qebehsenuef, with the head of a falcon, looked after the intestines. The goddesses Isis, Neith, Nephthys and Selket provided

RIGHT
(British Museum) A soul-bird,
representing the ba. *Faience, c.600*
BC.

extra protection to the canopic gods and to the coffin. In Ptolemaic and Roman times mummies were less well preserved; the organs were often left in the body and dummy canopic jars were used.

Strangely, also in the Ptolemaic and Roman periods, animal mummification became very popular and large cemeteries devoted to the appropriate animal were found close to certain cult centres. For example, ibises were buried at Hermopolis, the cult centre of Thoth, who was associated with the ibis.

Cats were mummified and buried at Bubastis where the cat-goddess Bastet was sacred. Exactly what was intended by this animal mummification is not clear, as research on the cat mummies shows that rather than dying a natural death, most had had their necks broken, and they consisted mainly of two groups – either young kittens or two year-old cats. Perhaps they were sent to serve the goddess Bastet in their after-lives.

The Egyptians believed that an individual was made up of five different elements: the physical body, the *ka*, the *ba*, the name and the shadow. At death the *ka* lived on and so required food and drink just as the body had done in life. This was supplied by the family of the deceased bringing food and drink to an offering-table at the tomb, or by making an endowment to a temple so that the priests could perform this function for them. In case this actual physical supply of offerings should cease, or in place of it altogether, the necessary offerings could be sup-

plied by magical means, by illustrating the offering process on the tomb walls, on the coffin, or on papyri placed in the tomb with the body. It was then believed that a kind of sympathetic magic would cause the event illustrated to happen.

The *ba* was the manifestation of the non-physical attributes of a person, and has sometimes been thought of as his soul, although this is not a strictly accurate equivalent. It is usually illustrated in the Book of the Dead and in other contexts as a bird with a human head and often with human arms, called a *ba*-bird or soul-bird. The *ba* was free to travel from the tomb by day, but it had to return to the mummy every night so that the physical body could survive in the afterlife. The *ba* travelled to the underworld to unite with the *ka* of the person to form the *akh*, which was the afterlife equivalent of the physical body of the deceased. Tombs had a false door that allowed the *ka* and *ba* to pass from the tomb to the world of the living and back again, and coffins had eyes painted on them so that the dead person could see out. These illustrate the strange mixture of abstract and concrete and of physical and mystical elements in the thinking of the ancient Egyptians.

One early notion of life after death was that the deceased rose to the sky and became one of the stars. A later idea, particularly bound up with the Osiris myth, was that the dead person carried on a life in the part of the underworld called the Field of Reeds in a manner similar to present life on earth. In the myth,

Osiris was killed and brought back to life again, eventually becoming ruler of the underworld. The texts and spells buried with the body were designed to help the resurrection into the afterlife, and to protect and guide the deceased person during the perilous journey through the underworld.

Before being placed in the tomb the mummy was placed in front of the tomb and the ceremony of Opening the Mouth was carried out in order symbolically to bring the mummy or dead person to life by means of rituals that would restore to it the power of speech, sight and the other senses. This ceremony was performed by the son or heir of the dead person, in the case of a king, by his successor. The deceased was also judged in the ceremony of the Weighing of the Heart in which the heart of the dead person was weighed against the Feather of Truth, which symbolized the *maat*, or sense of order and justice of the universe. The heart was chosen because the ancient Egyptians believed that the heart was the organ of

the intellect, transmitting its commands to all parts of the body via the bloodstream. These subjects are dealt with in more detail in the chapter on the Book of the Dead.

There are also a number of ancient Egyptian texts which are today known as 'Wisdom Literature'. Some of these are didactic in purpose, giving precepts for the conduct of everyday life, such as a father would give to his son, or a king to his heir. Others are more reflective in nature and are often called 'pessimistic' literature because they deal with the condition of order and particularly the disorder of the times they describe.

The earliest surviving didactic texts come from the 4th and 5th Dynasties and one, the *Instructions of Ptahhotep*, consists of the advice given by a senior state official to his son whom he wishes to succeed him when he retires from service. They include such maxims as:

'Consult the ignorant man as well as the wise one.'

24712

(British Museum) Wooden shabti-*box of Anhai showing Anhai and her soul-bird (*ba*) receiving refreshment from the goddess of the sycamore tree. The goddess is often portrayed as Hathor, but in this case she is shown as Nut.*

'If you abase yourself in the service of a perfect man, your conduct will be fair before God.'

'If you have been of no account, you have become great and if having been poor you have become rich and if you have become governor of a city, do not be hard-hearted because of your advancement, because you have become merely the guardian of the things which god has provided.'

'What is loved of god is obedience; God hates dis-obedience.'

A later text is the *Teaching of Amenemipat*, which is reminiscent of the Biblical Book of Proverbs. If there is any connection between this text and the Book of Proverbs, it is not certain which came first or which was the model for the other.

Examples of the reflective texts occur from the Middle Kingdom onwards, and these show a variety of philosophies which range from the deeply pes-simistic to the hedonistic. The *Song of the Harper* shows this latter view:

'Follow your desires as long as you live. Put myrrh on your head, clothe yourself in fine linen ...'

A later text says much the same thing:

'... cease not to drink, to eat, to get drunk and to make love. Make holiday, pursue your desire day and night.'

These texts give an insight into personal, reli-gious and ethical views quite different in character from those of the state religion, and demonstrate that many aspects of ancient Egyptian religion are not obvious on first inspection.

(National Archaeological Museum, Florence) Relatives bring food and offer incense to the dead. Painted limestone tomb relief.

CHAPTER FOUR
THE CREATION MYTHS

Creation myths are concerned with the moment at which the cosmos came into being and they attempt to elucidate for mankind, if only by creating a series of comprehensible images, the problem of how a force could exist within a state of non-being and how it could initiate the creation of a cosmos and its separation from the void. The images used in the detail of such explanations are naturally dependent upon the topography and circumstances of different areas of the world. It is not surprising that the dominant images in the Egyptian creation myths are water, a hill that rises from the water, and the sun that vanishes at night but rises each day to cross the sky once again.

There is no way of knowing how old such myths are, or in what form they were originally handed down orally from generation to generation. The first indications of such myths in Egypt are found in the Pyramid Texts from the late years of the Old Kingdom and the Coffin Texts from the Middle Kingdom. They had probably been in existence long before that, however, in a number of different forms, and ideas on the subject of creation probably affected pictorial language and ritual during the earliest period of the Pharaohs in ways we are unable to detect.

Our knowledge of the creation stories is derived from texts that have been influenced by the structuring of the myths by the priests at three chief centres, each of which was a cult centre for a particular deity. It is possible that political considerations played some part in the formulation of the myths as each centre in turn achieved importance and its priests attempted to locate significant events in the myths in their own area and relate them particularly to their favoured god. It should be remembered that alternative explanations or images that changed and developed over time were acceptable to the Egyptians, even when they were contradictory, and this is something to which the modern mind has to adjust. Nevertheless, in spite of the different ways found in the cosmogonies to express what are, after all, the very remarkable facts of creation, it will be seen that certain images are consistent.

The Cosmogony of Heliopolis

Heliopolis, the City of the Sun, was the name used by the Greek historian Herodotus for the Egyptian city containing the sanctuary of Yunu, which was a very important and very early temple of the sun-god. One of the most significant Egyptian cosmogonies, or creation myths, the one that later seemed to achieve perhaps the greatest degree of acceptance, was formulated there possibly about 3000 BC.

This tells us that in the beginning there was nothing but water. It was not merely an ocean or a lake with boundaries, but a limitless expanse of motionless water. It was called Nun. Even after the world was created Nun continued to exist at its margins and would one day return to destroy it and begin the cycle again.

By some unexplained means, a self-created god called Atum, 'The All', rose from the waters, even although they had no surface, and created the primeval mound of earth on which he could stand.

This primeval mound was important to all the cosmogonies and it has been suggested that it was an image that came naturally to people who were used to seeing such fertile mounds or islands reappearing after the obliterating flood-waters of the Nile had withdrawn, and that such a mound was possibly the inspiration for the building of the first pyramids.

In a sense, the priests of Heliopolis claimed the first land as their own in that they cherished a sacred stone called the Benben stone, alleged to be a relic of the event, that symbolized the primeval mound, where the rays of the first light of dawn may have struck and where a temple to the sun-god was built.

Because the creator, Atum, the All, as his name suggests, represented and contained within himself everything, he was able to create other deities from himself. Two explanations are given for the method by which he was able to induce life. The first says that he produced two children from his own semen by using his hand, which some versions of the story suggest may have represented the female principle also contained within him. The other explanation is

that he sneezed out the god Shu and spat out the goddess Tefnut. It is possible that there is a punning connection between the word Shu and the Egyptian word for sneeze.

Shu was a god of air, whose name comes from a root meaning 'empty.' His sister Tefnut, whose name may mean 'moist air', seems appropriately connected with spitting. In typically dualistic fashion, Shu was the air through which the sun shone, that is the kind of dry air that preserves things; Tefnut, on the other hand, was the kind of moist air that rots and corrodes.

The two deities were brought up by Nun, the waste of water, and watched over by the eye of Atum, which he could separate from his body. The eye, or *udjat*, plays a part in a story told about the childhood of Shu and Tefnut. Atum sent his eye to look for the children when they were lost from him in the wastes of Nun. Meanwhile he replaced it with a brighter eye, which was resented by the first eye when it returned with the children. Atum therefore placed the first eye on his forehead where it could

(British Museum) Nun, god of the primeval waters, holding the emblem of long life. His body is usually shown as blue or green, symbolizing water and fertility. Detail of the Papyrus of Ani.

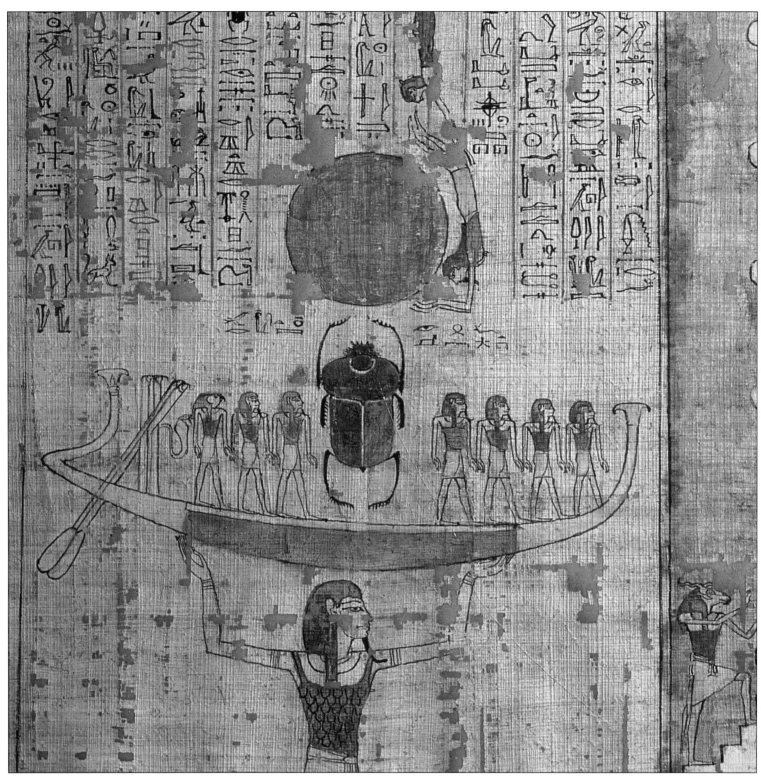

A detail from the Papyrus of Anhai which suggests both Creation and the daily rising of the sun. A god holds the boat of the sun containing the beetle-god Khepri (symbolic both of Creation and of the rising sun at dawn) and the red disc of the sun is received by the sky-goddess, Nut.

keep watch on the world once he had created it. Later, it became associated with the snake-goddess that was worn as the *uraeus* by the pharaohs on their foreheads. Another story says that he was so glad to see his children again that he wept for joy, and mankind was created from his tears.

The union of Shu and Tefnut produced two further deities – Nut, the sky goddess, and Geb, the earth god. It is interesting that Egyptian mythology is unlike Greek and other Indo-European mythologies in making the sky female and the earth male. Once again the brother and sister united to produce chil-

dren – the gods Osiris and Seth and their consorts, the goddesses Isis and Nephthys. From Nun had therefore sprung a family of nine gods, the so-called Ennead of Heliopolis, although Osiris and Isis also produced the god Horus in the next generation.

It seems possible that the priests of Heliopolis had at some stage grafted the generation of gods headed by Osiris on to the family of Atum in a deliberate move to connect the great god Atum's creativity with the gods of kings and men, and by doing this both to relate the kings of Egypt to the solar god and to reinforce the idea of the continual cycle of life and death in the universe that was so important in Egyptian thought. The myths concerning Osiris, which emphasize these notions, will be dealt with later.

Once Nut and Geb had produced their children, Shu separated them for ever. Illustrations show Nut, the sky, arching over Geb, the earth, who lies beneath her while Shu, the air, forces them apart, making space for himself. In doing this, he continued the creative principle of distinguishing and dividing the elements from one another.

By maintaining her posture, with her limbs at each cardinal point of the world, Nut creates a barrier to the waters of Nun. She is usually shown as a woman, decorated with stars, but is sometimes portrayed as a cow. It was said that every evening she swallowed the sun-god, Ra, who then travelled through her body at night to be born from her each morning, when the red sky suggested the blood caused by his birth. In an alternative account of the sun's journey, Ra travelled in a boat beneath her body by day and through the underworld at night.

At Heliopolis, the sun-god Ra was the cult deity, and aspects of Atum, 'the All', had been fused with him in several manifestations by the time of the Pyramid Texts. For example, the emerging sun was seen as Khepri, the scarab beetle, rolling the sun's disc before him just as the beetle propelled a ball of dung; the full, shining sun's disk was known as Ra, and the distant sun, was called Harakhti, the hawk. These names could be combined with the name of Atum, or Ra, the sun god as in Ra-Harakhti, for example.

Atum's birth as a sun god was also described in this set of myths by the image of a lotus flower that rose from the flood of Nun at the same time as the primeval mound. From the flower emerged a child who was the self-created sun god. In yet another image, the sacred bird of Heliopolis, the Benu-bird also acted as a manifestation of Atum as sun-god. The Benu-bird was associated with the benben stone, and their names may both be derived from the Egyptian verb *weben*, 'to shine' or 'to rise', which may also have suggested the otherwise mistaken

(British Museum) The dead Ani, portrayed as a swallow standing on a mound. This may refer to the primeval mound which rose out of the waters at the time of Creation, and to the benu bird which alighted on that mound. Detail from the Papyrus of Ani.

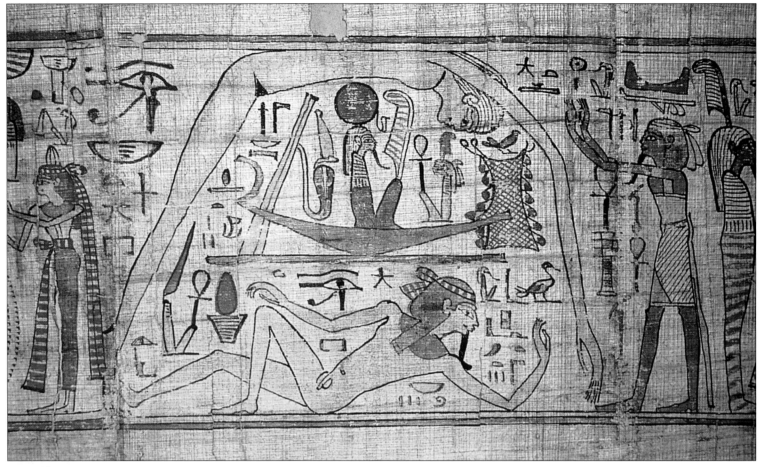

relationship Herodotus noted between the Egyptian bird and the Greek Phoenix. The bird is shown as a yellow wagtail in the Pyramid Texts and as a grey heron in the later Book of the Dead, but its association with the sun remains constant.

The Cosmogony of Hermopolis

Hermopolis is the Greek name given to the city in Upper Egypt that is known today as Ashmunein. It was earlier called Khmun, 'the Eight', for reasons that will become clear, and it was the cult centre of the god Thoth, the god of wisdom who is said to have given hieroglyphs to the Egyptians. The Greeks equated Thoth with their god Hermes, hence their name Hermopolis for the city.

The cosmogony developed at Hermopolis actually deals with events before that of Heliopolis because it concerns the nature of the featureless water before the act of creation, dealing with its negative characteristics, with what was not there before something was. It says that the waters either were, or produced out of themselves, four beings or deities and their female counterparts. These were Nun and Nunet, the primal waters; Heh and Hehet, whose name has been thought to mean infinity although it has also been suggested that it actually means the flood force inherent in water; Kek and Keket, darkness, and Amun and Amunet, whose name suggests a number of qualities: hiddenness, unseen energy, air

54

or wind. These eight deities were known as the Ogdoad, or Eight, of Hermopolis. The four gods were shown with frogs' heads and the goddesses with serpents' heads; thus they were perceived in the form of creatures who seemed to appear spontaneously each year from the mud and slime of the Nile's inundation.

It can be seen that Nun who, in the Heliopolitan myth, was himself the containing watery substance, is in the Hermopolitan myth only one element – the watery one – contained within the whole pre-cosmic substance. Of the other deities one, Amun, had the hidden potential energy to cause the disturbance that might have initiated creation from within the dark, inert waters.

By some means, a cosmic egg was formed within the dark waters, and when it broke light came from it. In some versions of the story, the cosmic egg was laid by a goose, the Great Primal Spirit in the form of the 'Great Cackler', whose cry was the first sound in the primal silence. It was probably a particularly local version of the story that claimed that the god Thoth in his form as an ibis flew to the primal mound with the egg. Again, there are two versions of what came from the egg: one says that Ra, in the form of a bird of light, hatched from it, another that it contained air which, once released, separated the sky from the earth and provided the breath of life for future creation.

In Hermopolis, this first burst of energy was also said to have thrust up a primeval mound, which was here described as the 'Isle of Flame' because the birth of the sun god there brought with it the first, flaming sunrise. Only later was the mound equated with Hermopolis itself.

Three pairs of the Ogdoad remained undeveloped and stayed where they were, being responsible for the flow of the Nile and the rising of the sun. Amun, the hidden, unknowable force was a different matter, however. His role as a creator grew more important, particularly in Thebes when it became a major religious centre later on. By a complex intellectual process of the priests, he was developed from being merely one of the elements present at the creation to being a transcendental force who created himself and actually energized the eight deities, of whom he was one, into the act of creation.

In Thebes he developed as the sun god, and can often be seen inscribed as Amun-Ra.

The Cosmogony of Memphis

The city of Memphis was built near the Nile Delta in about 3000 BC and deliberately developed as a political and religious centre, which doubtless felt the

need to compete with other centres like the ones already discussed. Its cult-god was Ptah, who had been worshipped in very early times as a supreme artificer, a great craftsman; later he was fused with Tatenen, which was the name given to the primeval mound, so that he was actually conceived, as Atun was in some of the versions of the Heliopolitan myth, as not only concerned in the creation of the mound, but as himself being it. His importance had, nevertheless, waned over the years. Evidence for the cosmogony formulated at Memphis comes from the so-called Shabaka Stone, on which was copied the contents of a much earlier text that has not survived.

It is in some ways the most interesting of the cosmogonies to a modern reader because it stresses intellect as a primary principle of creation. It claims

(Egyptian Museum, Cairo) The head of Tutankhamun as a child, emerging from the lotus flower is a symbol of the creation of the sun. From the tomb of Tutankhamun. 18th Dynasty.

Thoth, the ibis-headed god, leads Pensenhor to the underworld. Detail from the mummy-case of Pensenhor, from Thebes, c.900 BC.

that the god Ptah was the creator of the world, that he was also Nun, and that he created the Ennead, the nine gods of Heliopolis, with his heart and his tongue. To the Egyptians the heart is the seat of thought, the place where ideas are conceived, and the tongue controls speech and therefore the commands that determine action. Names were important to the Egyptians and, in a sense, the act of naming the gods would have given them life.

Ptah therefore created the other gods, including Atum, the first god of the Heliopolitan system, whose own acts of creation were simply the result of following Ptah's instructions. Ptah was thus responsible for the whole of creation, and present in it all. Having made the gods, he allotted them to places where they would be worshipped. He not only made the physical world, but also devised moral order, and he created political order in Egypt by devising the system of nomes or departments. He remained the great artificer and was, for that reason, equated by

others over the centuries. Behind them probably lie earlier stories and less developed great gods. They all suggest the overwhelming importance of the annual rise of the earth from the Nile's flood, and the daily falcon-like rise and fall of the sun that sometimes seemed to come too close to the earth. Behind them all is the sense that the flood waters are only just restrained, the whole process could start all over again, and the first act of creation was a wonderful moment that is constantly repeated in a less glorious fashion.

the Greeks with their god Hephaestus. But he was also 'Lord of Truth'. In Ptah, the priests of Memphis combined the intellectual force of creation by means of the word with the primeval mound itself, thus uniting mind and matter.

Khnum and the Creation of Mankind

The main cosmogonies are concerned primarily with the physical universe and with the chief gods, but the god Khnum concerned himself with making human beings. He was a potter, and thus a craftsman, like Ptah. Khnum was, however, depicted as ram-headed, having the horizontal horns of an early breed, and was thus associated with creativity among the animal world. His home was Elephantine at Aswan, in the cataract region of the Nile, where also lived Hapy, the god who controlled the annual inundation. Nile clay in that area provided material for potters, and the fertile soil brought Khnum a reputation for the provision of prosperity. At Esna, further north in Upper Egypt, Khnum was worshipped as the creator of all human creatures. Inscriptions there show in anatomical detail how he fashioned the human body, with its skeletal structure, its skin and internal organs. In him are combined the sources of animal energy, creativity and fertility, upon which life depends.

These have been merely summaries of some of the most outstanding Egyptian creation myths, and it is important to realize that they evolved and developed over time, that there are different, local versions of the myths and that some gods merged with

CHAPTER FIVE
THE MYTH OF OSIRIS

The myth of Osiris is one that developed and changed over the centuries as the god increased in importance and popularity. Stories about him were gathered into a complex myth that eventually wove together a number of important strands of Egyptian thought to form a pattern in which concepts of death and rebirth, order and disorder, vegetative growth and aridity, kingship and rightful inheritance were all balanced against one another and given a place.

His story has been pieced together by scholars from evidence found in many scattered sources from different periods, including the Pyramid Texts of the Middle Kingdom, inscriptions in temples and on stele, a variety of papyri, and the account of the Greek writer Plutarch. Consequently there are a number of versions of some incidents in the myth and the emphasis placed on certain events varies according to the period and the circumstances of their recording.

Although the first archaeological evidence for Osiris dates only from the middle of the 3rd century BC there is some reason to suppose that he existed earlier than that as a god of vegetation, having power over the germination and growth of grain crops in particular. The association between the god who lived on after death to rule in the underworld and the annual sowing of seed in the earth and the subsequent harvest is, in any case, a natural one. The continuity of his reputation as a god concerned with vegetation is confirmed by the 'Osiris beds' found in some tombs, in which a model of the god was filled with earth and sown with seeds that actually germinated inside the tomb. Naturally, new growth from the apparently dead seed was primarily meant in these circumstances to suggest his very strong association with the possibility of the rebirth of the dead in the underworld.

As the cult of Osiris increased in importance, he assimilated the natures of gods he replaced. At Busiris in the Delta, for example, he probably replaced the god Andjety, a royal god. It may be from him that he derived the royal insignia he is usually shown with: the crook and the flail and the high crown flanked by plumes, known as the *atef* crown. It will be seen that he became strongly linked with the notion of kingship.

He is said to have been born at Rosetau near Memphis, which was thought to have been the entrance into the underworld. At Abydos in Upper Egypt he assimilated the characteristics of the funerary deity, Khentiamentiu, and thus became known as 'Lord of the Westerners'. The name 'westerners' was given by the Egyptians to the dead because as the sun sets in the west each day it was thought to be the direction in which people also went at the end of their lives. From that time, Osiris was worshipped as a ruler of those buried in the cemeteries in the desert near Abydos, who would have hoped to enter the underworld successfully.

Thus Osiris had associations with vegetative fertility, with kingship and with rule over the underworld. We have already seen how the cosmogony of Heliopolis brought the god into connection with the

sun god in his manifestation as Atum by making Osiris his grandson, the eldest child of Nut, the sky goddess, and Geb, the earth god. By doing this, it also linked the older gods to mankind through the role of Osiris as king.

Some of these complexities are expressed in visual representations of the god. He is shown as a man with kingly attributes, but is wrapped in the bandages of a mummy; because of this his body is often white, but sometimes it is black like the mud of the Nile or green like reborn vegetation.

As we have seen, Osiris had two sisters, Isis and Nephthys, and a brother, Seth. One source says that Osiris and Isis fell in love in the womb. All agree that they married, thereby providing a pattern of royal marriage between brother and sister.

Following the rule of the god Shu, succeeded by his son Geb, Osiris became king and he and Isis presided wisely over the kind of golden age commonly found in mythological descriptions of a remote period. Crops grew well, the climate was tempered by breezes, there was order on earth and people behaved justly to one another.

This peaceful episode was brought to an end by the rulers' younger brother Seth, who slew Osiris in order to seize power for himself. It was said that Seth had always represented violence and disorder, to the extent that he had begun life by tearing himself from his mother's womb. Even his pictorial representations suggest his disorder; he is shown as a probably mythical animal, with the long, downward-curving nose of an anteater, and unique upward-pointing, squared-off ears.

The earliest sources of the story of the death of Osiris suggest a reluctance by contemporary Egyptians to dwell on the murder of a reigning king; they merely say that the 'Great One' fell on his side on the bank of the Nedyet river; sources from the Middle Kingdom, however, say directly that Seth attacked and killed him on the river bank.

Osiris's sister and wife, the goddess Isis, sought sorrowfully for her husband and, having found him, she 'gathered up his flesh', possibly preserving his body magically from corruption. From that point, Osiris became ruler of the underworld, or *Duat*.

A much fuller version of the murder of Osiris was recorded well over a thousand years later by Plutarch. It is thought that, although he imposed a Hellenistic influence on the myth, for example by calling the Egyptian gods by their corresponding Greek names, he recorded its current outline accurately enough from the sources he consulted in Egypt, and that the earlier story would inevitably have changed by that date. Plutarch tells the following version of the story.

He begins with an account of the conception and birth of Osiris, saying that at the moment of his birth a voice was heard to say that the lord of creation was born. He describes his period as king of Egypt, emphasizing his devotion to the civilizing and teaching of his people. After his success in Egypt he went on a journey to teach other nations of the world. On his return, the envious god Seth (whom Plutarch calls Typhon, after a monster of Greek mythology) gathered together 72 like-minded comrades and a Nubian Queen, who plotted together to kill Osiris.

They managed secretly to measure his body exactly. Seth invited Osiris to a banquet with other guests. During the feast, some of the conspirators brought a beautifully wrought chest into the hall, suggesting that it might be a gift for the man who best fitted inside it. Osiris took his turn at lying in the chest, which of course fitted him exactly. Seth's followers instantly closed the chest, sealing it with molten lead. They then took it to one of the mouths of the Nile and threw it into the river so that it might be carried away into the sea.

The chest came ashore near Byblos on the coast of Lebanon by the roots of a young tamarisk tree which swiftly grew, enclosing the chest within its trunk. The flourishing tree came to the attention of the king of the country, who ordered it to be cut down to be used as a pillar in his house. While the tree had been growing, Isis had been searching desperately for her husband. When she heard about the wonderful tree, she went to Byblos herself.

She gained entry to the palace by becoming

(Louvre) Osiris, Horus and Isis. Gold and lapis-lazuli. 22nd Dynasty.

LEFT
(British Museum) Osiris-Khentiamentiu. Wallpainting from a Theban tomb c.1200 BC. Osiris as the god associated with the necropolis of the west, and as ruler of dead souls.

OPPOSITE
Statue of Horus at his cult temple at Edfu. He is shown as a falcon wearing the crown of Upper and Lower Egypt, symbol of his mythical kingship of the land after the death of his father, Osiris.

nurse to the king's newly born son, whom she suckled with her finger. In a desire to make him immortal, she put him into the fire each night so that his mortal parts might be burnt away. One night, while this was happening, she had changed herself into a swallow in order to sing out her lamentations. The queen came to listen and, appalled by what she saw,

pulled her son from the flames.

Isis told the queen her story and begged successfully to be given the pillar. She retrieved the chest from inside it, and her cries of grief killed the child she had been nursing.

She took the chest to Egypt where she opened it and hid it in the marshes of the Delta. One night,

Osiris thus served as the first example of the body preserved skilfully enough to ensure the preservation of life after death. He entered the underworld, where he lived on to supervise the judgment of those hoping to enter into eternal life after death. He was often thought of as the underworld counterpart to the sun-god, bringing some share of light to that dark place. Although Osiris and Ra were sometimes perceived as 'Twin Souls', there was occasional rivalry between them and Osiris was sometimes perceived as malevolent. There was no doubt of his power, however.

To return to earth, Isis was now pregnant with the son she had wanted to conceive as the inheritor of the kingdom formerly ruled by Osiris, although there are versions of the story that say she had given birth to a son while Osiris was still alive. The more common versions of the story, however, that describe Isis conceiving her son from the revived corpse of her husband, emphasize the maternal care and guile of Isis as she prepared to give birth to the future heir and to watch over his infancy so that he might grow up to challenge Seth and retrieve his father's kingship from him.

Some sources say that Seth imprisoned Isis, jealous of the honours she had done to the body of Osiris, and that the god Thoth, who acted as the vizier of Osiris, helped her to escape. Most agree that she made her way secretly to the papyrus swamps of the delta to prepare for the birth of her child.

The son she bore to Osiris was the god Horus, the hawk. The myths concerning his growing up to adulthood and his eventual recovery of the kingship, as we shall see, help to explain his complex character as a god. He contains the notion of vulnerability because of his representation at times as a child; his eyes, vital to the falcon, are important in his story, and are sometimes thought of as the sun and the moon; perhaps most importantly, his successful striving for just and rightful kingship lay behind the fact that all Egyptian kings were perceived as the manifestation of the god Horus, and for a long period kings used 'Horus' as the first of their titles.

Once Horus had been born, Isis watched over him, but had to leave him from time to time to find food. On one of those occasions, Seth discovered the child and turned himself into a poisonous snake in order to approach him through the swamp. When Isis returned she found her son near death, suffering from the snake's poisoned bite. She appealed to the surrounding people for help but, although they gave her their sympathy, no one knew a spell strong enough to defeat the poison. She realized Seth was behind the

when she had left the chest unattended, Seth discovered it. He took out the body of Osiris and cut it into 14 pieces, which he scattered throughout Egypt. When Isis heard what had happened she set out with her sister Nephthys, who could not tolerate Seth's action even though he was her husband, and they eventually gathered together the scattered fragments of the body except, says Plutarch, for the phallus, which had been eaten by a fish.

Other Egyptian sources say that the whole body was recovered. Some say that the goddesses buried each part where they found it, thus accounting for the growth in the Osiris cult in certain places. Other sources say that Isis gathered the body together and breathed life into it. She is shown in one illustration hovering over Osiris in the form of a bird, a kite, fluttering her wings to create the breath of life. Because she did this, Osiris revived for long enough to impregnate her. By this means she conceived their son Horus. After this she used her skills to preserve the body of her husband and bind it in linen, and she performed rites that ensured he would have eternal life.

attack, and the episode is presented as the first of a number of attacks by Seth upon Horus, and one in which evil threatens innocence.

Isis called upon the great god for help, and the sun's boat stopped near her so that the god Thoth could descend from it and hear her plea. Thoth spoke on behalf of the sun god and promised that the boat would stop its course, bringing darkness and death to the world, until Horus was cured. The great threat worked as a powerful spell, and Horus was saved. Thoth told the sun-god, Ra, that his son had been saved, for indeed Horus was descended from Ra, or Atum. In this story it can be seen that the people expressed their support and sympathy for the young son of the king, and that the greatest god demonstrated that the world would collapse if any harm came to him. It thus gives cosmic significance to the concept of kingship.

Isis protected Horus herself after this; she is often shown nursing a baby, and there is a reference in the Pyramid Texts to the ruler drinking milk from her breasts. When young, Horus was known as 'Harpa-khered', Horus the Child, from which the Greeks constructed the name Harpocrates by which he is more commonly recognized in the west. He is often pictured at this age sitting on his mother's knee, with his shaven head dressed with the so-called sidelock of youth, although at times he is shown as an innocent force capable of keeping away dangerous creatures, for example when he stands on the back of a crocodiles holding snakes in his hands.

A number of myths developed around the goddess Isis, most of which emphasized her maternal nature, her guile and determination and her skills in magic, all of which were necessary to bring her son to successful maturity on her own.

She was often referred to in spells used to cure children from illnesses resulting from the kind of accidents that naturally occurred to them – snake bites and scorpion stings, falls, burns and so on. She is shown to have a special connection with snakes and scorpions. In one story, she went to visit the Town of the Two Sisters in the Nile Delta, taking with her seven scorpions whom she warned to be discreet so that they did not draw the attention of Seth to the group. A wealthy woman, seeing them approaching her house, barred the door to them, but a poor peasant woman invited them in, offering hospitality as people should.

Six of the scorpions gave their poison to the seventh, who slid into the first house and stung the son of the wealthy woman. Her inhospitable nature was repaid when no one answered her cries for help. Isis,

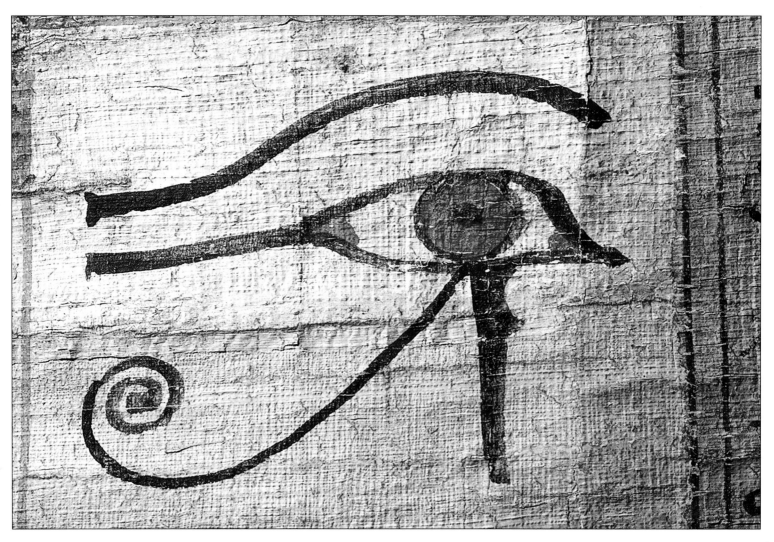

nevertheless, was unable to refuse help to a suffering child, and cured him with a powerful spell in which she named each scorpion in turn so that she had power over them and their poison, which then became harmless. The woman, in her gratitude, shared her wealth between Isis and the poor woman who had sheltered her.

The greater aspirations of Isis are illustrated by the story of her attempt to take a senior place among the gods when she tired of living on earth as a woman. She determined to discover the secret name of Ra, which she knew would give her power over him so that she could persuade him to help her. She had noticed that saliva sometimes dribbled from the mouth of the ageing Ra. She modelled a poisonous snake from a mixture of some of his saliva and the dust into which it had fallen, then she put the snake where Ra would be sure to walk on it. When the snake bit him, Ra became extremely ill and was unable to help himself because the damage had been done by a creature he had not himself created.

Isis asked if she could help relieve his terrible pain, saying she would overcome it with her spells if he would reveal his name to her. At that, he declared a long list of his many public names, including Khepri in the morning, Ra at midday and Atum in the evening. These did not satisfy Isis, however, for none of them was his hidden name, the one that would give her power over him. When he was persuaded that he would not be cured unless he did as she asked, he withdrew from the other gods and caused his name to pass directly from his heart to hers, forbidding her to reveal it to anyone other than Horus. Then she cured him. The papyrus in which this story is told does not reveal the secret name of Ra, but it does give the spell used by Isis, which could be used by anyone needing a cure for the sting of a scorpion.

In this myth lies an explanation of the way in which the great power of the supreme sun-god passed to the younger family of gods, of which Osiris was the head, and so to future rulers of Egypt, descendants and manifestations of Horus.

Horus eventually arrived safely at adulthood, when he was known as Har-wer, Horus the Elder, or Haroeris in Greek. It was time to make his claim to the kingdom of Egypt and to displace his uncle (in some versions his brother) Seth from power. He went to a tribunal of the gods, presided over by Ra. His great-grandfather Shu, the god of air, supported his claim at once, and Thoth, the god of wisdom, agreed with him. Isis thought all was well and prepared to send the good news, on a wind, to Osiris in the underworld.

At that point Ra intervened to say that he had not yet agreed. When Thoth pointed out the legitimacy of Horus's claim in view of the fact that Osiris was his father, Ra indicated that Seth's great strength perhaps gave him a better claim to rule. It has been suggested that such practical considerations might suggest that the kingship myth is rooted in a real struggle for power early in Egyptian civilization, but there is as yet no evidence for the idea.

It has to be remembered here that Seth was also a complex character, who was chaotic, violent and evil, but who was nevertheless venerated in certain parts of Egypt. Ra supported him as ruler, not only because he was older and stronger than Horus, but also because Seth travelled in the prow of the sun-boat, being the only god who could deal with the serpent Apophis who tried to swallow the sun each evening as it crossed the western horizon.

At the tribunal, Seth characteristically suggested that he and Horus should go outside and settle the matter in a trial of strength, but Thoth restored order and the matter remained unresolved for 80 years. The patience of the tribunal being exhausted, they sent to the great goddess Neith for her advice. She was absolutely decisive in her view that Horus should inherit the throne directly from his father, but sensibly suggested that Ra should console Seth by offering him two of his daughters, Anat and Astarte, as wives. These were goddesses who had entered Egypt from the Middle East during the New Kingdom.

In spite of the tribunal's willingness to accept this advice, Ra refused and soundly abused Horus in a very personal way, emphasizing his youth, weakness and general unsuitability as a potential ruler. A comparatively junior god taunted Ra with his unpopularity and Ra left the tribunal. His good humour was restored when his daughter, the goddess of love, Hathor went to him, showed him her naked body and somehow contrived to make him laugh. He returned to the tribunal and asked Seth and Horus to make their claims to the throne once again.

Seth made his usual claim of strength and of his ability to hold chaos at bay by his attacks on the serpent Apophis. Horus reiterated his legitimate claim through his father Osiris. Isis, losing patience, intervened on behalf of Horus and so infuriated Seth that he threatened to kill the gods in turn, one each day. He said he would take no part in any court into which

Isis was allowed. Ra then removed the tribunal to an island. He ordered the ferryman, Nemty, not to bring across to the island any woman who looked like Isis.

Naturally enough, Isis used her magic skills to disguise herself as an old, poor woman. She placed a gold ring on her finger and carried a bowl of flour with her to the ferry. When Nemty refused to take her across, she pleaded that she needed to go to the island to take food to a young man who had been there for five days tending cattle, and who must be very hungry by now. Finally, the ferryman agreed to take her in return for her gold ring, having refused the cake she first offered him.

When she arrived at the island, Isis chose a moment when the gods were relaxing to make her approach. She changed herself into a beautiful young woman and made sure that Seth could see her. He was instantly attracted and went to talk to her. She threw herself on his mercy, playing her role as a young widow whose son was being threatened by an intruder who intended to take from him the cattle that had belonged to his father and to seize his home. Seth expressed great indignation at this behaviour, putting himself on the side of the son and against the intruder. Isis changed herself once again, this time into a bird, a kite, so that she could keep at a safe distance from Seth. From the branch of a tree she told Seth how he had condemned his own behaviour to Osiris and Horus by his words.

Seth, in tears, reported all this to Ra, who could not find it within himself to be too sympathetic. Showing the unpleasant side of his character, Seth demanded that the ferryman, Nemty, should be brought to the tribunal. It was decided that, because of his disobedience, Nemty should have his toes cut off.

After that incident the court moved once again, this time to the Western Desert, where it decided that the throne of Egypt should go to Horus. The decision was held up once more, however, when Seth demanded that he should challenge Horus to a series of personal contests for the throne. This resulted in a number of bizarre encounters between the two gods.

In the first, Seth suggested that each of them should change himself into a hippopotamus and submerge himself under water for three months. Whoever came to the surface during that time would lose his claim to the throne. After a time, Isis could not contain her concern for what was happening to her son under water so she made a harpoon, which she threw into the water at the point where the beasts had submerged. Unfortunately it first hit Horus and she had to remove it with a spell. When she succeeded in harpooning Seth, he appealed to her as his sister and, unable to resist the argument, she removed it from him, too.

Her action infuriated Horus, who surged from the water and cut off the head of his mother, which he took with him into the mountains of the desert, where it became a headless flint statue. When Ra heard of the action, he vowed that Horus must be found and punished for it. It was Seth who found Horus as he lay asleep by an oasis. He took out the eyes of Horus and buried them, but they grew into lotus blooms. After his savage action, Seth returned to Ra, claiming not to have seen Horus, whom he assumed would by then be dead.

The goddess Hathor found Horus and magically healed his eyes by rubbing them with the milk of a gazelle. In a different story, Seth stole the left eye of Horus, the moon, in revenge for being castrated. In that story too the eye was healed. In both cases the eye of Horus, always referred to in the singular, became stronger, in a sense perfected, by the healing process it had been through. For that reason, representations of it were often used as an amulet, a protective symbol.

At some stage Isis was restored to herself, and she played a part in the next contest between Seth and Horus. Seth invited Horus to a banquet in a gesture of apparent reconciliation. During the evening Seth made a homosexual attack on Horus which Horus ingeniously avoided, catching Seth's semen in his hand. When Horus showed the semen to Isis, she cut off the polluted hand, making him a new one. Then she took semen from Horus, which she spread on lettuces growing in the garden, knowing that Seth would eat them because he was particularly fond of them.

Seth then went to the court of the gods and claimed that he had taken Horus homosexually. The gods expressed their contempt of Horus for allowing himself to be dominated in this way, but Horus demanded that the gods should summon the semen of the two men. When Thoth called on Seth's semen it did not come from Horus but from the waters of the marsh; the semen of Horus emerged as a gold sun disk from the head of Seth.

Even then, Seth devised another contest, in which the two men would build ships of stone in which to race one another. Horus built his of wood, but coated it in plaster to make it look like stone. Seth made his from a whole mountain peak. In the contest before the gods, Seth's boat naturally sank, so he turned himself into a hippopotamus and broke up the boat of Horus. Horus was prevented by the gods from killing Seth in his rage and frustration and went instead to the sanctuary of the goddess Neith to

ask her why he could not gain his inheritance when all the right seemed to be on his side.

The problem was finally resolved when Thoth persuaded Ra to write to Osiris in the underworld, addressing Osiris in flattering terms and giving him a fully royal title. Osiris and Ra disputed their rival powers, Osiris emphasizing his role in feeding the gods with wheat and barley, a claim about which Ra was dismissive. Osiris finally persuaded the other gods of the power of his position by pointing out that everyone came over the western horizon and into his realm in the end.

Then the gods decided as one that Horus should indeed succeed his father as ruler, and he was established on the throne of Egypt. Ra compensated Seth by giving him a place in the sky where he could enjoy himself noisily as a god of storms and thunder. Other versions of the story, however, say that Seth was banished to the desert margins of the country, and so stress his aridity compared with the fertility represented by Osiris.

The Osiris cult was associated with the death of the king and the establishment of a new king when his predecessor passed into an assured life in the underworld. It set the pattern whereby Horus reigned after the rebirth of Osiris into eternal life. As time went on, the cult of Osiris became more popular; it was possibly a myth that people could relate to their own lives, sympathizing with the story of a man who had suffered injustice and attained eternal life through the ministrations and care of a loving wife. In this respect Osiris may have seemed closer to them than most of the other gods; it is interesting, too, that the stories about Isis sometimes concern ordinary people.

Men hoped to achieve eternal life, and they saw Osiris as the means by which they might do it. To this end, at the period when the habit spread further through society, they copied the embalming that had saved him, seeing the process itself as a way of sharing in his suffering. It even became habitual to preface the name of the deceased with the name 'Osiris'.

Although they feared Osiris as a judge of souls, it seems that over time they came to find him more approachable and relevant to their lives than the more remote sun god, whose cult was chiefly the province of monarchs and priests.

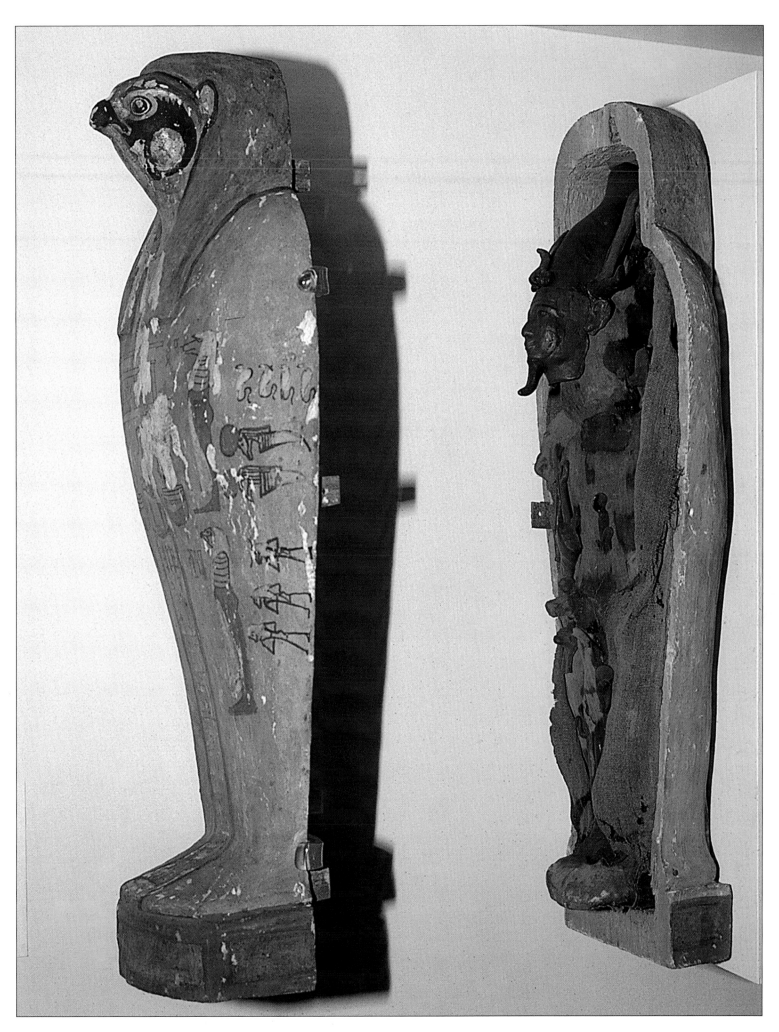

CHAPTER SIX
THE BOOK OF THE DEAD

The scribe, Ani, stands with his hands raised in adoration before an offering table bearing meat, fruit, loaves, cakes and flowers. Behind him stands his wife, Thuthu, a priestess-musician at the Temple of Amun, holding a sistrum and a reed in her left hand.

The name Book of the Dead is applied by Egyptologists to a collection of spells that were placed with a burial to help the deceased person to gain entry to the afterlife, and to pass through the dangers of the underworld to reach a new existence in the Field of Reeds. The ancient Egyptians would have called it something like 'Spells for Coming Forth by Day', which refers partly to the need for the *ba* to be able to leave the tomb and assume different forms outside it. In all, there were over 200 spells but they do not all occur together in any one example. Instead, a selection would be made according to the choice of whoever was ordering the book, and was probably dependent to some extent on the amount of money available to pay for it.

The texts were usually written on papyrus, on a roll up to 41m (135ft) long in the case of the longest one so far discovered and up to 48cm (20in) high. Sometimes the texts would be written on the coffins or on the tomb walls or on linen or vellum, but papyrus was the usual medium. The papyrus would then be placed on or near the mummy, or even be incorporated in the mummy wrappings. Often, the papyrus roll would be placed in a hollow part of a special statuette of the god Ptah-Sokar-Osiris.

Texts of the kind found in the Books of the Dead first occurred as the Pyramid Texts, which decorated the walls of the royal pyramids at Saqqara in the 6th to 8th Dynasties (the first example of the Pyramid Texts is found in the pyramid of King Unas, the last king of the 5th Dynasty). Many of the spells use archaic language and refer to a stellar heaven. The idea that the dead would become stars around the pole star is a much earlier belief than the one held by the occupants of the pyramids, namely that they would journey to the sky and there join the sun-god in a solar kind of afterlife. This suggests that they were originally composed at a date far earlier than that at which they first appear. They also refer to the later Osiris cult, and include the Ceremony of Opening the Mouth, which are prominent in the Book of the Dead texts a few centuries later.

As burial customs became 'democratized' and the practice of elaborate burials spread down from the kings to the nobles and richer subjects, there arose a new form, known nowadays as the Coffin Texts, which were painted on the inside and outside of coffins. These became popular in the Middle Kingdom period, and they continued to describe two kinds of afterlife: the deceased might go to the sky to join the company of Ra, or they might go to the underworld to the kingdom of Osiris. In addition to the necessary spells, a plan of the underworld would often be painted inside the coffin to guide the occupant on his journey.

During the New Kingdom, from about the mid-15th century BC, examples of the Book of the Dead appear. Now the emphasis is on Osiris as the king of the Underworld where the dead will live for eternity. Osiris is also the judge of the dead, and a whole section is devoted to the judgment process, including the Weighing of the Heart. The texts also illustrate the belief that in the afterlife, in the Field of Reeds,

Anubis prepares the mummy of Ani. The mummy lies on a bed, and wears the false beard with upturned end, as worn by the divine mummy of Osiris. The jackal-headed figure attending to the mummy may be regarded as either the god Anubis himself, or as a priest wearing an Anubis mask.

the familiar agricultural tasks would have to be carried out as on earth, hence the need for *shabti* figures to deputize for the dead person and to do his work. Spells were needed to bring these models and figurines to life, and to make them do the work when called upon. These spells would often be written upon the *shabti* figures as well as recorded on the papyrus scroll. There were also spells designed to keep the body whole, such as the spell to prevent him losing his head in the realm of the dead. Many of the spells rely on the magic power of knowing how to name someone; often this would be a minor god or doorkeeper at some gate through which the dead must pass.

The production of the Book of the Dead texts must have become quite thriving industry for the scribes and illustrators. The texts were written in cursive hieroglyphic, hieratic or demotic scripts, and illustrated by vignettes, which could be in full colour or simple black-and-white outlines. Often the vignettes and the scripts were produced by different people, and sometimes different sets of scribes and illustrators would work on different sections of the book, joining them up later to make a continuous roll. Some of the texts were regarded at the time they were copied as being very ancient and mysterious

and difficult to understand, and mistakes were often made in the copies. Sometimes sections would be repeated in error, or illustrations would not be appropriate for the adjacent text. Often the vignettes would be drawn first, and the text filled in later, and sometimes not enough room would be left between the drawings for the text to fit in, so parts would be omitted. There could also be great unevenness of quality: a particular book could have excellent drawing and very poor quality text, and vice versa. The book would usually be made to order, according to whatever spells were considered appropriate or necessary, or what could be afforded. The name of the dead person would be incorporated into the text as the book was produced, but sometimes books were produced beforehand with spaces left for the names to be filled in later when a customer was found.

The details that follow are mostly from the Book of the Dead of the scribe Ani, from Thebes, dated about 1250 BC. He was an accountant and manager of the granaries of the lords of Abydos and a scribe of the lords of Thebes. His wife Thuthu was a noble lady who was also a musician-priestess of Amun-Ra and she is shown in the vignettes carrying a musical instrument, the sistrum. The papyrus is about 24m (79 ft) long, and after the first quarter of its length the

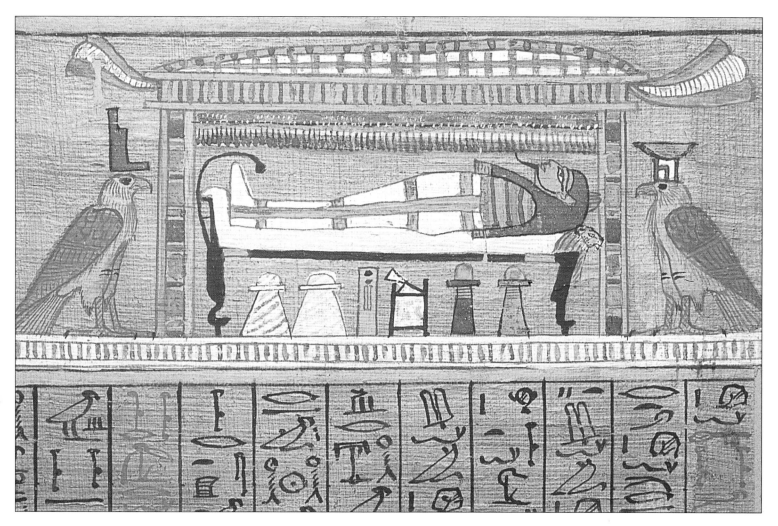

name of Ani has been filled in, which suggests that the papyrus was bought from stock, and only the first part was individually produced for Ani. There are over 200 spells, and a selection of them are listed below.

For coming out into the day.
For going out into the day and living after death.
For not doing work in the land of the dead.
For have a shabti *work for one in the land of the dead.*
An appeal to Thoth to speak for him at the tribunal of the gods.
To open the mouth of the deceased.
For not permitting his heart to be taken from him.
For not letting his heart speak against him in the judgment.
To prevent him losing his head in the land of the dead.
For not putrefying in the land of the dead.
To drive away a crocodile who comes to take away his magic.
For protection against being bitten by a snake in the land of the dead.
For breathing air and having power over water in the land of the dead.
To allow transformation into any shape desired.
For being transformed into a lotus.
For being transformed into a swallow.
For bringing a ferry-boat in the land of the dead.
For embarking on the boat of Ra.
To worship Osiris.
To escape from the Catcher of Fish.
For not dying again.
To leave yesterday and to come into today.

The spells themselves are repetitive and rely heavily on the magic of naming. A paraphrase of the spell for being changed into a benu bird runs like this: '*I came into existence from unformed matter, I created myself in the image of Khepri and grew in the form of plants. I am made out of the essence of all the gods.....I am crowned, I become a shining one, I am strong and holy among the gods. I am the god Khonsu who drives back all who oppose him.*' Or the spell for being changed into a lotus reads: '*I am the pure lotus who comes forth from the god of light, the guardian of the nostrils of Ra, the guardian of the nose of Hathor. I come forth and hasten after him who is Horus. I am the pure one who comes forth from the field.*'

The mummy of Ani lying on a bed in the form of a lion. Under the bed are a scribe's palette and some containers. Two kites stand as guardians at each end of the bed. The kite at the foot represents Isis, as shown by the throne-shaped headdress. Nephthys stands at the head of the mummy; her headdress is the hieroglyph for gold.

Detail of the Papyrus of Ani. This vignette accompanies a hymn to Osiris. Isis and Nephthys adore the sun-disc which is held aloft by an ankh, *symbol of life, which stands on a* djed *pillar. This takes place beneath the blue vault of the sky, bounded by the mountains of the Eastern and Western horizons. The baboons are shown adoring the sun because they chatter and are active at sunrise; they are regarded as wise animals associated with Thoth.*

Another, perhaps more practical, spell is the one for not dying a second time, which meant to die for all eternity, whereas after the first death there was a chance of eternal life if one passed the judgement. Parts of the spell are perfectly understandable as the fears and wishes of a person facing death. *'What kind of land have I come to? There is no water, nor air, it is deep and unfathomable, black as night and men wander helplessly here. In here a man cannot live in peace of mind, nor can the longings of love be satis-*

fied here. But let the state of the shining ones be granted to me for water and air and for satisfying the longings of love, and let peace of mind be given to me as food and drink ... may my heir be strong, may my tomb and my friends who are left upon the earthn flourish and may my enemies be destroyed. I am your son and Ra is my father. For me you have also made life, strength and health. Horus is established upon his throne...' (The deceased person lives again in the form of Horus) *'...he shall wear the atef crown for* millions and hundreds of thousands and tens of thousands and thousands and hundreds and tens of years; bread, ale, oxen, wild fowl, all good and pure things and clear water shall be offered to him in abundance...'

This spell was to be recited over a figure of Horus made of lapis-lazuli and placed near the neck of the mummy; it would give him power on earth over men and the gods, and if recited in the underworld it would be most beneficial.

Perhaps the most interesting spell is the one that accompanies the vignette of the Weighing of the Heart. Part of it today is called the Negative Confession. In it the deceased addresses the members of the tribunal one by one and declares his innocence of wrong-doing. It starts like this:

'Hail, you whose strides are long, who comes forth from Ammu, I have not done iniquity. Hail, you who are embraced by flame, who comes forth from Kheraba, I have not robbed with violence. Hail, Fentiu, who comes forth from Khemennu, I have not stolen. Hail, Devourer of the Shade, who comes forth from Qernet, I have done no murder, I have done no harm...'

Always the greeting comes first, then the statement of lack of guilt. It is still interesting today to see what was deemed to make up a life free from sin in ancient Egypt. Some of the sins enumerated in the negative confession include:

I have not defrauded offerings, I have not

Ani and his wife are shown as two soul-birds representing their bas. On their heads are thought to be perfume cones, but it is not known for certain what they are.

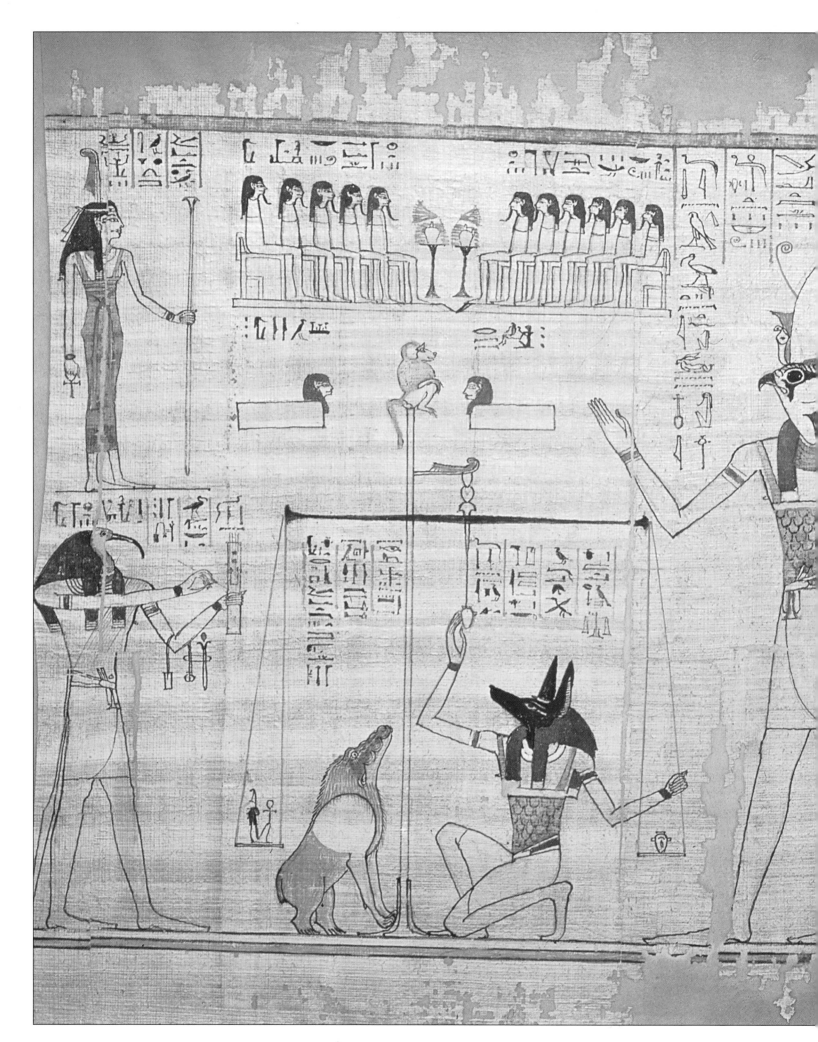

diminished oblations, I have not plundered the god, I have spoken no lies, I have not snatched away food, I have not caused pain, I have not committed fornication, I have not caused shedding of tears, I have not dealt deceitfully, I have not transgressed, I have not acted guilefully, I have not laid waste the ploughed land, I have not been an eavesdropper, I have not spoken evil against anyone, I have not defiled the wife of any man, I have not been angry without just cause, I have not polluted myself, I have not stopped my ears against words of right and truth, I have not acted with insolence, I have not stirred up strife, I have not judged hastily, I have never cursed the king, I have never fouled the water, I have never cursed God, I have not stolen, I have not plundered the offerings of the blessed dead, I have not filched the food of the infant nor have I sinned against the god of my native town, I have not slaughtered the cattle of the god, I have not behaved with arrogance, I have never magnified my condition beyond what was fitting.

Here we seem to have an insight into the moral aspirations of the ordinary person at the time, and a closer understanding of the values and practical requirements that controlled behaviour at the time. Even here, this section ends, in some of the texts at least, with an invocation which brings back the sense of magic in naming that occurs in many myths in all parts of the world. The dead person has to pass through the Hall of Two-fold Maat:

'I will not let you enter over me,' says the bolt of the door, 'unless you tell me my name.' 'Weight of the Place of Right and Truth is your name.' 'I will not let you pass by me,' says the right post of the door, 'unless you tell me your name.' 'Weight of the Labours of Right and Truth is your name.' 'I will not let you enter in by me,' says the left post of the door, 'unless you tell me my name.'

'Judge of Things is your name.' 'I will not let you pass,' says the threshold of the door, 'unless you tell me my name.' 'Ox of Seb is your name.' 'I will not open to you,' says the bolt-socket of the door, 'unless you tell me my name.' 'Flesh of His Mother is your name.' 'I will not open to you,' says the lock of the door, 'unless you tell me my name.' 'The Utchat of Sebek, the Lord of Bakhan Liveth is your name.' 'I will not open to you and I will not let you pass over me,' says the dweller at the door, 'unless you tell me my name.' 'Arm of Shu that Protects Osiris is your name.' 'We will not let you pass by us,' say the posts of the door, 'unless you tell us our names.' 'Serpent Children of Rennut are your names.' 'You know us, pass by us.' 'You shall not

Horus leads Anhai to the judgement where the ceremony of the Weighing of the Heart is taking place. Anhai's heart is in a small container on a balance, being weighed against Truth in the form of a small effigy of Maat, goddess of truth, distinguished by the feather on her head. Anubis supervises the weighing, and the monster Ammut waits to devour any heart which fails the test and is therefore unworthy of proceeding to the afterlife. Thoth, ibis-headed, stands to the left, recording the result, and the baboon sitting above the scales is also symbolic of Thoth. Beyond Thoth stands Maat, goddess of order and truth wearing the Feather of Truth and holding an ankh. Above the scales sit eleven gods who are witnesses to the judgement.

tread on me,' says the floor of the hall, 'unless you tell me my name.' 'I am Silent, I am Pure.' 'I know not the names of your two feet with which you would walk upon me; tell them to me.' '...before Amsu is the name of my right foot and Grief of Nephthys is the name of my left foot.' 'Tread upon me, because you know me.'

The vignettes shown here are also mostly taken from the Book of the Dead of the scribe Ani, from Thebes, dated about 1250 BC. Other illustrations are taken from the Papyrus of Anhai, who was a priestess-singer of Amun-Ra at Thebes, dated about 1150 BC, and from the Papyrus of Hunefer, who was an overseer and royal scribe in the palace of Seti I in the 14th century BC. These two papyri appear to have been made specially for each person. Later examples come from the Saïte period, when the Book of the Dead was extensively revised and the sequence of the spells, or chapters, was regularized. This form was popular from the 26th Dynasty until the end of the Ptolemaic period. The Papyri of Ani, Anhai and Hunefer are all now in the British Museum.

Other funerary texts were also used, both on the walls of pyramids and tombs and on papyri. The texts are called by such names as 'What is in the Underworld', 'The Book of Gates', 'The Book of Caverns', and 'The Book of the Secret Dwelling'. Even as late as the Ptolemaic period, new works of a similar nature were being produced, designed to protect the dead person and help him on his journey to the underworld. These include 'The Book of Spending Eternity' and 'The Book of Breathing'. They demonstrate a remarkable continuity of thought over centuries, but also show an increasing reliance on individual righteous behaviour as a qualification for attainment of the afterlife.

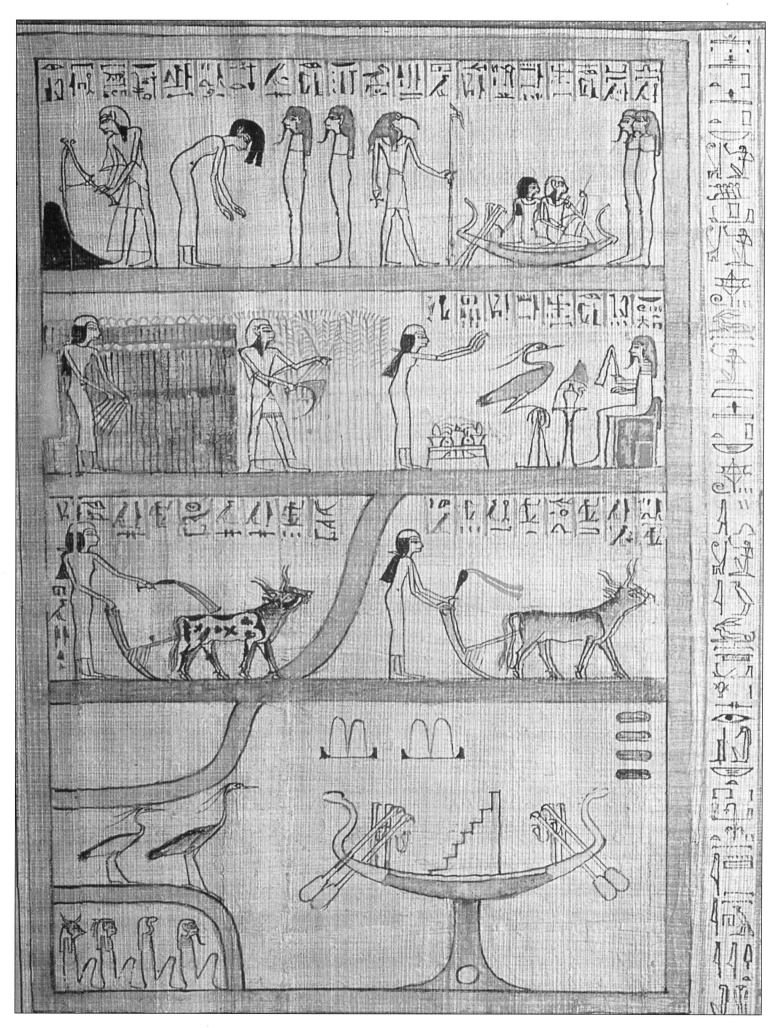

CHAPTER SEVEN
THE GODS OF ANCIENT EGYPT

AHMOSE NEFERTARI (c.1575-1505 BC)

Queen, wife and sister of Ahmose I and mother of Amenhotep I, she outlived her husband and was regent during her son's reign, and apparently outlived him too. She was later deified as one of the divine guardians of the necropolis of Thebes, and was especially revered at the village of Deir el-Medina, where the workmen of the royal tombs of the Valley of the Kings lived, and which was founded by Ahmose Nefertari and Amenhotep I.

AKER

An earth-god who controlled the junction of the western and eastern horizons in the underworld, he is usually shown as two lions seated back-to-back.

AMENHOTEP I (Amenophis I) (1525-1504 BC)

Second ruler of the 18th Dynasty, son of Ahmose Nefertari and, like her, he was later deified as a guardian of the Theban necropolis.

AMENHOTEP SON OF HAPU
(c.1430-1350 BC)

He was Scribe and Chief-of-all-the-Works of Amenhotep III. He had cult chapels in temples at Deir el-Bahri and Deir el-Medina, and was worshipped for his wisdom, as a scribe and for his powers of healing.

AMMUT

Underworld goddess with the head of a crocodile, foreparts of a lion andrear of a hippopotamus. Known

as the Devourer of the Dead, she is usually shown in the Book of the Dead beside the scales in the ceremony of the Weighing of the Heart, waiting to devour the hearts of those who fail the test and are not fit to pass into the afterlife because of their past deeds.

AMUN (Amen), Amun-Ra,

Originally a local deity at Thebes, usually shown in the form of a ram, he became the major deity of Egypt when the Theban kings of the 11th Dynasty rose to power. His position as the supreme god of Egypt was strengthened by assimilating with the sun-god Ra to become Amun-Ra. As Amun Kanutef he was a fertility god like Min, and was portrayed as an ithyphallic figure. He was the father of the Theban triad of gods, his wife being Mut, a local goddess, and their son the moon-god Khons. The great Temple of Amun at Karnak was his main centre, administered by a rich and powerful priesthood and visited by many pilgrims. The cult of Amun lost power temporarily when Akhenaten transferred his capital to El-Armarna and worshipped Aten. The supreme position was soon regained but declined when the Assyrians destroyed Thebes in AD 664 and the cult of Osiris became more popular and influential. Regarded by the Greeks as the equivalent of Zeus, the cult of Zeus

Ammon spread to Greece, and then as Jupiter Ammon his cult spread to the Romans.

ANUBIS

A god of the dead in the form of a dog or jackal. The jackal was an animal of the Western Desert, and so became associated with the domain of the dead, in the west. Later, the cult of Anubis became associated with that of Osiris, and Anubis was then said to be the son of Osiris and Nephthys. Anubis embalmed the body of Osiris and carried out the funerary rites for him. In the Book of the Dead, Anubis is the god who supervises the embalming and mummification process, who protects the mummy, is present at the ceremony of the Opening of the Mouth, and who performs the Weighing of the Heart. Anubis is also associated with the Imuit fetish, which is a headless, stuffed animal skin hanging from a pole standing in a pot. The Imuit fetish is often illustrated on stelae or papyri, and a model of it was found in the tomb of Tutankhamun, but its function is not known.

ANUKET (Anukis)

Goddess from Nubia whose cult centre in Egypt was in the region of the First Cataract. Khnum, Satis and Anuket formed the Elephantine triad.

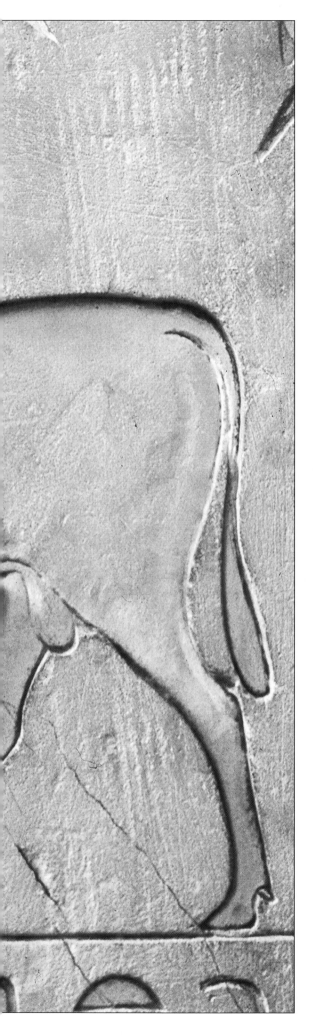

APIS

A sacred bull who was regarded as a manifestation of Ptah. At intervals a new Apis bull was born, black and bearing special markings that included a white mark on the forehead and the image of a vulture on its back. The new bull would be brought to his cult centre near that of Ptah at Memphis and the old bull would be ceremonially drowned in the Nile. The body of the old bull was mummified and buried in a splendid granite sarcophagus in an underground cat-acomb known as the Serapeum at Saqqara, a short distance from Memphis. The dead bull became iden-tified with Osiris, and was known as Osiris-Apis or Osorapis.

APOPHIS (Apep)

An underworld snake deity, personifying darkness, evil and chaos, Apophis attacks the boat of Ra as it travels through the Underworld each night, and is defeated, but never destroyed. Seth protects the boat of Ra and subdues Apophis, using force and magic to do so. Although Seth is shown as the enemy of Apophis, he later became identified with him, as a symbol of forces hostile to the order of the gods.

ATEN

The deity represented as the sun's disc, and empha-sizing the beneficial aspects of the sun. It is shown as a disc with many rays stretching out like arms, end-ing in hands, some of them presenting the ankh, sym-bol of life, towards the king. Aten appeared in the record as a god around 1500 BC in the reign of Thuthmose I and slowly gained prestige during the 18th Dynasty. Amenhotep III favoured Aten, and priests of Aten became established at Heliopolis, the centre of the cult of the sun-god Ra. When Amenhotep IV became ruler, he made Aten the prin-cipal god and built the Per-Aten Temple at Karnak, close to, and in competition with, the Temple of Amun.

Five or six years into his reign, Amenhotep IV founded a new city to the north beside the Nile, about midway between Thebes and Memphis. He called this Akhetaten, meaning The Horizon of Aten, known today by its Arabic name of El-Amarna. At the same time he took the name of Akhenaten ('glory of Aten') in place of Amenhotep ('Amun is con-tent'). Akhetaten became the new capital. Two new temples were built, not roofed as in the traditional temple design, but open to the sun. Aten was made the supreme deity of the state, but it is not possible to prove that this was a a complete conversion to monotheism. The religion was also exclusive in that

(Louvre) The bull-god Apis wearing a sun-disc between its horns.

RIGHT
(British Museum) Bronze figure of Bastet holding an aegis (broad neck-decoration) in her left hand.

OPPOSITE RIGHT
(British Museum) Bronze cat sacred to the goddess Bastet. Bronze, Roman period.

BELOW
(British Museum) Head from a large figure of the god Bes. Blue faience, c.100 AD.

only the king or his queen, Nefertiti, could have direct access to Aten. Akhenaten reigned for only 18 years, being succeeded briefly by Smenkhkare (Nefernefruaten) and then by Tutankhaten, who may have been the younger brother or the son of Akhenaten. Tutankhaten was married to Ankhesenpaaten, one of the daughters of Akhenaten, but the couple changed their names to Tutankhamun and Anhkesenamun, and dissociated themselves from the cult of Aten. The capital was moved back to Memphis and within a few decades the city at El-Amarna was abandoned. Many reliefs showing Akhenaten or Nefertiti were defaced, to erase them and their heresy from the record.

ATUM

The creator-god of Heliopolis who 'came into being of himself' among the primeval waters of Nun. He created Shu (air) and Tefnut (moisture), who became the parents of Geb (earth-god) and Nut (sky-goddess) whose children were Osiris, Isis, Seth and Nephthys. These were the family of the nine gods (or Ennead) of Heliopolis. Atum is usually shown in the form of a man, wearing the double crown.

BASTET (Bast)

Cat-goddess whose cult centre was Bubastis; as a daughter of the sun-god she personified the beneficial aspects of the sun's power, contrasting with the savage aspects attributed to Sekhmet. Bastet was shown with the attributes of a lion in the early period, but after the Middle Kingdom she was shown as a woman with a cat's head, and took on a more protective, friendly aspect. As a mother-goddess she is often accompanied by kittens. She is also often shown carrying a sistrum, which suggests association with Isis and Hathor.

BES

Bes was usually shown as a dwarf-like figure, with a grotesque bearded face. He may originally have been a lion-god, because he has a lion's tail, ears and mane, although it is not clear whether they are his own members or part of a lion-skin which he may be wearing. He was a protective spirit, helpful in keeping snakes away from houses, and generally warding off evil spirits. He would be present at a birth, dancing, singing and playing a tambourine or drum to frighten away evil. Bes became increasingly popular in the later period, and many domestic items such as mirrors, toiletry items, perfume jars, and beds bear his image. He acted also as a protector of the dead, as his image often appears on the disc-shaped head-rests of mummies.

His consort was Beset, depicted as a female dwarf, or as a snake, but he was also thought to be married to Taweret, a goddess of childbirth. Unlike other Egyptian gods, who are nearly always shown in profile, Bes is usually shown full-face. This may be because he could have originated outside Egypt, in the Sudan.

DUAMUTEF – see Sons of Horus

EDJO (Udjat)

The cobra-goddess of the Delta, with a cult-centre at Buto, Edjo was shown as a snake or a woman wearing the red crown of Lower Egypt. She was represented as the *uraeus* cobra worn on the forehead of the Pharoah in a menacing attitude to defend the king against his enemies.

GEB

The earth-god who appears in the creation myth of Heliopolis, the brother and husband of Nut, the sky-goddess, and the son of Shu, god of air, and Tefnut, goddess of moisture. His children were Osiris, Isis, Seth and Nephthys. Geb judged between Horus and Seth and made Horus, as the rightful heir of Osiris, ruler of the living, and from this came the pharoah's right to rule. Geb as the god of earth is a vegetation and fertility god: water and plants spring from him.

But for the dead he was a malevolent god, imprisoning the buried ones within his body. One ancient myth makes Geb and Nut the parents of the sun, and therefore the ancestors of all the gods. Geb is also seen as a goose, the Great Cackler, which laid the cosmic egg from which the sun was born.

HAPI (HAPY)

The god of the inundation of the Nile and one of the Four Sons of Horus, Hapi is portrayed as a man with pendulous breasts to emphasize his fecundity, and with papyrus or lotus plants on his head. His body is often shown coloured green or blue. He lived among the caverns in the rocks at the First Cataract and one of his main cult centres was near Aswan. Some temples show many figures of Hapi bearing offerings, again an indication of his role as fertility god.

HARPOCRATES

Horus as a child appears as a young boy with the sidelock of youth and his finger to his mouth. He is also shown gaining mastery over serpents, scorpions and crocodiles, and in the Greek and Roman periods images of him were set up in houses to protect the family from these creatures, and to ward off evil spirits. In the Osiris-Isis-Horus myth he was attacked as a child by snakes sent by Seth but overcame them.

HATHOR

Goddess of joy, love, fertility, music and dance, and daughter of Ra, Hathor was a sky-goddess like Nut, with whom she was often confused or assimilated. She appears in the form of a cow, usually bearing the sun-disc in her horns, or as a woman with the ears of a cow. As goddess of music and dance she carries a sistrum, a rattle-like musical instrument. Besides being regarded as the daughter of the sun-god, she was also regarded as the mother of Horus the Elder by Ra, and as the wife of Horus of Edfu. As the mother of Horus she was also regarded as the mother of the reigning king, and has been shown as a cow suckling the Pharoah. Her main cult centre was at

(National Archaeological Museum, Florence) The goddess Isis wearing the cow's horns and sun-disc associated with Hathor.

Dendera, where a huge temple was dedicated to Hathor in Ptolemaic times. From this temple at Dendera Hathor would make an annual journey by boat up the Nile to visit her husband Horus at Edfu, and this became a popular and joyous festival and pigrimage.

She was known as the Lady of the Sycamore in Memphis, and appears on many funerary objects as a cow-headed lady leaning out of a sycamore tree supplying food and drink to the deceased person. In a funerary context she was called the Lady of the West and received the setting sun each evening, protecting him on his nightly journey through the underworld. The dying therefore sought her protection, and in the Book of the Dead she stands as a cow on the slopes of the Western Mountain to protect and nurture the dead.

Hathor, as a benevolent deity, was popular at all levels from king to common person, and the great temple at Dendera, which was built in Ptolemaic times and continued to be enlarged in Roman times up to the reign of Trajan, shows that her popularity continued until late times. However, as the Osiris-Isis cult gained prestige and popularity, Isis usurped many of the features of the cult of Hathor and often appears as a combined Isis-Hathor figure.

HEH

One of the Ogdoad (group of eight primeval deities) of Hermopolis, Heh is the god of infinity, and by extension of this concept he appears on royal regalia as a charm to ensure longevity.

HEKET (Heqat)

A goddess in the form of a frog, associated with birth and re-birth. In the Pyramid Texts she helped the dead king on his journey to the sky. As the consort of Khnum (who made the first humans on his potter's wheel) she gave life to the figures which he fashioned, and as a goddess of childbirth it was believed that she shaped the child in the womb and gave it life.

HORUS

From earliest times the falcon was worshipped as a god of the sky and as a sun-god. As a sky-god, his eyes were the sun and moon. As the emblem of victorious leaders in predynastic times, the falcon became associated with the king, who was regarded as the earthly manifestation of Horus. As the sun-god Ra was also a powerful symbol of the king's might, Horus became identified with the sun too. The falcon must have been a popular symbol of power in early

times as there were many independent cult-centres dedicated to the falcon as god of the sky. With time, the different cults were brought into the cult of Horus, but remained as variants of the main Horus cult. Consequently the mythology of Horus is very complicated, and as with other Egyptian deities, their stories can be confusing and sometimes contradictory.

IMHOTEP

A historical figure, he was a courtier who held high office under King Djoser, or Zozer, in the 3rd Dynasty. He is credited with designing the Step Pyramid at Saqqara, the first stone building on such a scale. So great was his reputation that, very unusually, he was deified about 2,000 years after his death. Bronze figurines of him show him seated with a papyrus scroll open across his lap. He became credited with healing powers, which caused the Greeks to identify him with their healing god, Asklepios. He was also thought to be the son of the god Ptah, and was thus the focus of prayer by those who hoped he might be able to transmit his father's creative force.

IMUIT FETISH SYMBOL

This took the form of the skin of a headless animal that had been stuffed and hung on a pole. The pole stood in a pot. Although it is recorded as early as the 1st Dynasty, it became particularly associated with the worship of Anubis, and is sometimes thought of as his fetish or as one of his attributes.

IMSETY – see Sons of Horus

ISIS

A very powerful and popular goddess, Isis was one of the children of Nut and Geb and the devoted sister and wife of Osiris. The hieroglyph of her name represents a throne, and her name might actually have meant that. She became particularly associated with the throne of Egypt because she and Osiris were the first rulers in a golden age, and she became the mother of Horus, and therefore of all subsequent Egyptian kings. She breathed life into Osiris after his murder by Seth, and is often shown in the form of a kite, whose wings hover protectively over her husband. She protected her son, Horus, from the machinations of Seth until he was able to take his rightful place on the throne.

Isis was credited with particularly magical powers and great tenacity. She became closely associated with cures for children's ailments, especially

those caused by the bites and stings of snakes and scorpions. From the period of the New Kingdom, the *tyet* amulet became particularly associated with her. This was a girdle knotted in a certain way, which possibly has some connection to the *ankh*.

Because of her strongly maternal qualities, she could be presented as a sow. She was also sometimes shown as a cow, which perhaps accounts for her occasional confusion with the goddess Hathor. Her cult became extremely popular beyond the confines of Egypt in the Roman period.

KHENTIAMENTIU

Both Osiris and Anubis are described as Khentiamentiu which means 'foremost of the Westerners' to show their status over the necropolis, which was usually to the west of the Nile. An earlier canine deity at Abydos was called Khentiamentiu, but his cult was superseded by Anubis.

KHEPRI

The sun god as a creator, represented in the form of a scarab beetle. This was the name given to the sun-god as he appeared above the horizon in the early morning at the start of his daily journey, presumably an analogy with the beetle that rolled a ball of dung before him all day. The dung beetle was also an appropriate image for the creator and sun god, Atum, because from the ball of earth, containing its eggs, a new beetle appeared to emerge spontaneously. Although he is a comparatively early god, amulets in the form of a scarab appear most frequently from the Middle Kingdom.

KHNUM

A ram-headed god whose cult was centred mainly on the island of Elephantine at Aswan from about 3000 BC. He was strongly associated with the annual inundation of the Nile, which he was thought to supervise. This, together with his powers as a ram, made him one of the creator-gods. His creativity was expressed through the pottery he made, and he is sometimes represented sitting before a potter's wheel on which he is turning a newly-created human figure. His aspect as a potter was particularly evident in his cult centre at Esna, where he was celebrated as creator of gods, people, animals and fish.

KHONS

His name means the 'traveller' because he was a moon god, who travelled across the sky. He is usually shown in mummy-like clothing that binds his legs together, and wears on his head the full moon held within the crescent of the new moon. Like other moon gods, he was associated with the baboon, and his early character was fierce. Later, at Thebes, he was seen as the son of Amun and Mut, and sometimes shown as a child wearing the sidelock of youth. In this aspect he shared the characteristics of a protector against violent animals with Horus in his aspect as a child.

MAAT

A goddess who personified the laws of ordered existence, harmony, justice and truth both in a cosmic sense and among the society of men. She wears an ostrich plume on her head, which was sometimes used on its own to signify her. The hieroglyph used for her name shows the plinth on which her seat rested, and it may also have signified the primeval mound where life began. As well as order on earth, she represented the order in the universe that resulted from the moment of creation. Quite late in her development she became known as 'Daughter of Ra'.

In funerary papyri she is often shown at the

judgment of the dead when the deceased's heart was balanced in a pair of scales against her feather to determine his suitability to enter the afterlife. It has been said that her effigy was worn by officials when they presided in Egyptian law-courts.

MENTU

A falcon-headed god of war. He is usually shown wearing a headdress formed from a sun-disc and two plumes. His cult centred on Thebes from about the 11th Dynasty, when some of the kings used the name Mentuhotep, meaning 'Mentu is content', but his cult there gradually gave way to that of Amun. His strength lay in fighting the enemies of the gods and he saw to it that the kings of Egypt were victorious over their enemies. Therefore he came to symbolize the more aggressive aspect of the pharaohs. In the later period he was associated with a black-faced white bull called Buchis, who came to be regarded as an earthly manifestation of the god.

MERETSEGER

A local cobra-goddess of the mountain overlooking the Valley of the Kings at Thebes. Her name is usually translated as 'She who loves silence', which seems appropriate for one who watched over a great necropolis. She was particularly venerated by workers in the valley, who have left inscriptions on stones

(British Museum) Funerary stela showing the fertility goddess Qadesh, standing on a lion between the fertility god Min and Reshuf, an Amorite war-god.

attesting to her power to strike down with blindness or snake poisoning all those who committed crimes, and indicating that she could also offer cures to the repentant.

MESHKENT

Goddess of childbirth, identified with the kind of birth brick that Egyptian women squatted on to give birth. Sometimes she is shown as such a brick with a female head, at others as a woman with a brick on her head. As a funerary goddess, she helped the deceased to be reborn into the afterlife, and she was therefore present at the judgment of the dead. She was also thought to have had a hand in determining the destiny of a child at birth.

MIN

God of male potency and of fertility. His early emblem, somewhat resembling a bolt of lightning, has proved impossible to interpret. His representation as a man cannot, however, be mistaken. He is shown standing with his legs together and with an erect phallus protruding at right angles. In his right arm, which is held up away from his body and bent at the elbow, he holds a flail that rests on the finger-tips of his right hand in a way that has been thought possibly to suggest sexual penetration. On his head he wears a crown surmounted by two very tall plumes, and a long ribbon from the crown hangs down his back. He seems to have been an early agri-cultural god who retained his characteristic of ensur-ing prolific harvests and fecundity in general by means of his sexual potency. He is sometimes shown with offerings of cos lettuces, which appear to have been a symbol of potency, perhaps because of their shape but more possibly because of the milky sap that is reminiscent of semen. Pharaohs in the New Kingdom took part in festivals in honour of Min as part of the ritual intended to celebrate the fruitful renewal of the kingship.

MUT

A Theban goddess who is shown as a woman, usual-ly wearing a brightly-coloured dress. On her head she wears a headdress shaped like a vulture, above which is placed the combined crown of Upper and Lower Egypt. She carries the papyrus or lily sceptre of Upper Egypt. She was so important at Thebes that she replaced Amunet as the wife of Amun, and thus became, like the other important mother-goddesses, Isis and Hathor, the symbolic divine mother of the earthly king. The child of Mut and Amun was Khons. When Amun was perceived as the sun-god Ra, she became the eye of Ra and was presented as a lion-headed goddess because that is how the eye of Ra was normally manifested. Because of this she began also to be associated with the cat and was therefore fused with the cat-goddess Bastet as Mut-Bastet.

NEFERTEM (NEFERTUM)

The god of the primeval lotus blossom that rose from the waters of Nun at the beginning of creation and from which, in one version of the myth, the sun first rose. He is described in the Pyramid Texts as the bloom 'held to the nose of Ra'. He is some-

(British Museum) Head of the goddess Nut wearing the headdress of Hathor. Faience.

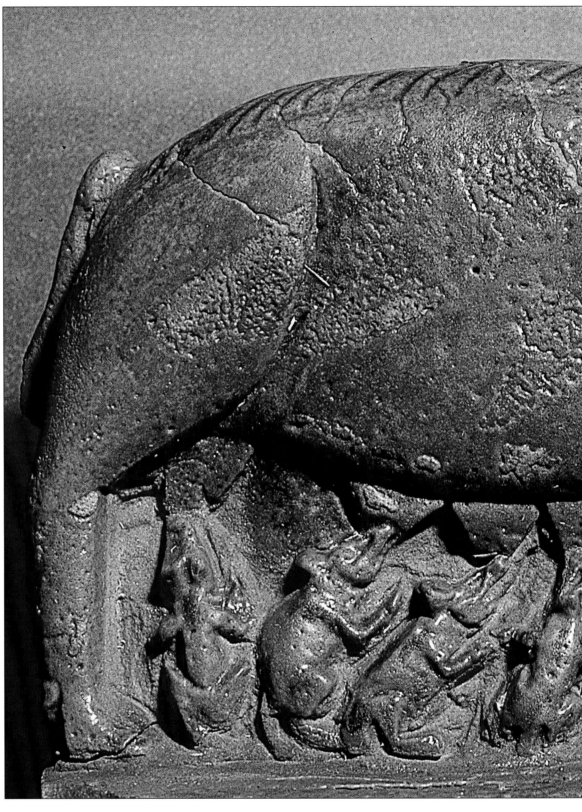

times equated with Horus as the child of the sun. He is usually presented as a man wearing a lotus-shaped headdress, sometimes decorated with two plumes. At other times he is shown with a lion's head, and at Memphis he was thought to be the son of the lioness goddess, Sekhmet.

NEITH

A very ancient creator goddess, whose cult was centred on Saïs in the Delta. Her earliest emblem was a shield with crossed arrows, and she is commonly shown wearing the red crown of Lower Egypt. By the period of the Old Kingdom she had become the consort of the god Seth and their son was the crocodile god Sobek. At various periods her important role as a creator was stressed, and she was even said to have invented birth. She was one of the four goddesses who watched over the bier of Osiris. Her funerary role centred on the linen coverings of the mummy, for she was thought of as

(British Museum) Sow and piglets, sacred to the sky-goddess Nut. Faience, Saïte Period, c.600 BC.

the mythical inventor of weaving.

NEKHBET

A vulture goddess whose local importance grew so that she came to represent Upper Egypt in the same way that Wadjet, the snake-goddess represented Lower Egypt. The vulture and the snake came to symbolize the two halves of the country, and were used in the royal insignia for that purpose. Nekhbet was often shown as a vulture with spread wings who clasps the symbols of eternity in her claws. She can also be a protective symbol, when she has one wing stretched out before her. Her chief function was as a mother-goddess and as a protective nurse to the king.

NEPHTHYS

A goddess of the Ennead of Heliopolis, one of the four children of Geb and Nut. To balance the marriage of Osiris and Isis, she is said to have married her brother Seth. In the Osiris myth she nevertheless

95

supports Isis sympathetically in her struggle against Seth. She accompanied Isis when she escorted successive monarchs to the underworld, weeping for them as she had done for her brother Osiris.

NUN

The god who contained within himself the waters of nothingness from which the creator-god emerged in the creation myths. Although he was known as 'father of the gods', this stresses his antiquity rather than his real position. Once Atum, the sun-god, had risen from the waters of Nun, Nun himself had no role to play except in his continued existence that implied the possibility that he could overwhelm the cosmos once again. He was also thought of as beneficent when his name was given to the sacred lakes within temple enclosures.

NUT

The sky goddess of the Heliopolitan creation myth. She was the sister of Geb, the earth, with whom she had four children: Osiris, Isis, Seth and Nephthys, before being separated from him by Shu, the air. She is shown arched across the earth, with her hands and feet at its four cardinal points, and thereby she holds at bay the chaos from which the cosmos had evolved. She was also thought of as the mother of Ra, the sun-god, because she swallowed him every evening and he travelled through her body at night to be born again from her body in the morning. She was also therefore perceived as a funerary deity, receiving the body of the king into her embrace. She came to be represented on the underside of coffin lids, where she arched her body over the deceased who might hope to be born again from it after re-enacting the sun's journey.

ONURIS

A god of hunting who was also a sky god sometimes identified with Shu, the air. He is usually shown as a bearded man holding up a sword and wearing four tall plumes.

OSIRIS

One of the most important gods of Egypt. He was probably an ancient god of fertility, who was associated with corn and with the cycle of its burial in the earth as seed, its resting time in the dark beneath the earth and its germination or resurrection to life. As his importance grew, he assimilated characteristics of other gods whom he displaced. He was strongly connected with kingship and is usually shown carrying the royal insignia of crook and flail. He was the son of Nut and Geb and the first king of Egypt. He was killed by his envious brother Seth, but restored to life by his wife Isis for long enough to impregnate her with a son, Horus, who eventually recovered his kingdom. The skills of Isis preserved him so that he was restored to life in the underworld. He ruled there, supervising the entry of the newly-deceased into his kingdom, and there he represented the sun in its night-time aspect. He became a symbol of the resurrection into life and was seen as such by the many followers of his cult.

PTAH

The creator god whose cult centre was Memphis. He is usually portrayed as a man dressed in a close-fitting garment; his head is shaven and he wears a tightly-fitting skull cap. In his hands he holds a staff that is a combination of the ankh sign and the sceptre of straightness and stability. From the period of the Middle Kingdom he is shown with a straight beard. He was above all the god of craftsmen, and was thought to have created skills in metal-work and sculpture. Consequently, Imhotep, who created the Step Pyramid, came to be thought of as his son. In the creation myth devised at Memphis, perhaps in rivalry to that of Heliopolis, he is said to have created the world by the thoughts coming from his heart and the words from his tongue. During the Old Kingdom his cult merged to some extent with another deity of Memphis, the hawk-god Sokar, and from this combination emerged the funerary god Ptah-Sokar. Naturally enough, this deity gradually assumed the attributes of Osiris, the god of the dead, and emerged as Ptah-Sokar-0siris, images of whom were often included among the funerary objects of private people.

QADESH

A goddess of Middle-Eastern origin who was introduced into Egypt in the New Kingdom and became part of a triad with the gods Min and Reshep. She was a goddess of sexual pleasure, and is usually shown as a naked woman holding out flowers while she stands on the back of a lion.

QEBEHSENUEF – see Sons of Horus

RA (RE)

The creator sun-god of Heliopolis, which was his chief cult centre. He is usually represented as a falcon wearing the sun's disc on its head, which in its turn is surrounded by the body of the snake-goddess that symbolizes his death-dealing powers. When he

the Fayum. In the course of time he became assimilated into the cult of Amun and worshipped as another manifestation of the sun-god.

SOKAR
See Ptah

SONS OF HORUS
These were the four deities who were responsible for protecting the internal organs of the deceased once they had been put into canopic jars. Their roles became defined over time and the stoppers of the canopic jars were then made in the forms of the heads of each of the gods. Human-headed Imsety was responsible for the liver; ape-headed Hapi was responsible for the lungs; jackal-headed Duamutef was responsible for the stomach, and falcon-headed Qebehsenuef was responsible for the intestines.

TAWERET (TAURT, THOERIS)
A hippopotamus-goddess who protected women in childbirth. She was said to have been the concubine of Seth but to have gone over to the side of Horus in the dispute between them, thus showing her kinder nature. She can be shown with the head of a hippopotamus, the legs and arms of a lion, the tail of a crocodile and the pendulous breasts of a mature woman – an appearance that was meant to deter malevolent forces from harming women in labour, and one that did not prevent her from being a very popular goddess with the ordinary people of Egypt.

TEFNUT
The sister of Shu. They were the first gods produced from the body of Atum.

THOTH
A moon-god who was responsible for knowledge and writing, and who was particularly venerated by scribes. He had two forms – a baboon and an ibis – probably because at some stage he had become assimilated with another god. In papyri he is sometimes shown in his ibis-headed form recording the results of the weighing of the heart of the deceased, but he was also thought of as guardian of the dead, helping them to find their way in the underworld.

TRIADS
The word triad is used to describe a group of three gods. The three are usually perceived as forming a divine family of father, mother and son, who were all venerated as a group at a particular cult centre. The constitution of the triads sometimes seems forced as it was clearly a convenient way of bringing together gods who had earlier had an independent existence in an area. Among such triads were Amun, Mut and Khons at Thebes, Ptah, Sekhmet and Nefertem at Memphis, Khnum, Satis and Anuket at Elephantine. Osiris, Isis and Horus formed the most familiar triad, but each was actually worshipped at an independent centre.

WEPWAWET
A jackal-headed god whose name meant 'opener of the ways', which could refer both to the conquests of rulers and to the entrance to the underworld, for he sometimes helped the king in battle, but he also performed the ceremony of the Opening the Mouth of the king at his burial and lead him into the underworld.

CHAPTER EIGHT
GREEK, ROMAN AND COPTIC EGYPT

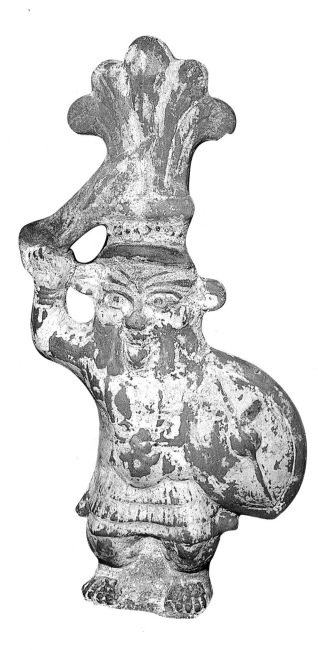

Under the Ptolemies the city of Alexandria, on the Mediterranean coast, became established as the capital and grew to be an important centre of trade and learning. There had already been a significant population of Greeks in Egypt before Alexander the Great, and during the rule of the Ptolemies more Greeks came to Egypt, to trade and to settle, and their influence increased, particularly in the Delta and in the Fayum.

The Ptolemies encouraged Greek culture, so that Alexandria became the major centre of learning in the Mediterranean world during Hellenistic times. At the same time, however, as pharaohs they encouraged the Egyptian priesthood, restored many temples and founded a number of new ones.

Ptolemy I introduced the cult of Serapis, combining Egyptian and Greek gods into one deity, and he established the main cult centre, the Serapeum, at Alexandria. Serapis was formed from the fusion of the Egyptian gods, Osiris and Apis combined with the Greek gods Zeus, Hades, Asklepios and others. This was brought about as a deliberate attempt to retain the elements of Egyptian religion while adding those of Hellenistic Greece, and was largely successful. Not only was the cult popular in Egypt, but it spread to other parts of the Hellenic and Roman world, and a cult centre to Serapis was even set up on the sacred Greek island of Delos in the 3rd century BC. Serapis was a god who could be all things to all people and nations, for he represented the solar, fertility, healing and funerary aspects of divinity. Usually he is shown with a corn measure on his

At first, funerary customs continued the ancient Egyptian tradition, and even the early Coptic funerary art retains references to Anubis, the *ankh* and other symbols. Mummification was still practised during the Roman period and mummy portraits show a delightful fusion of traditional Egyptian art with the Hellenistic style.

The cult of Isis had increased in popularity in the later dynasties of ancient Egypt, and continued to do so during Ptolemaic times. Under the Romans it spread throughout the empire. A temple of Isis was found under the ashes which covered Pompeii, and artefacts relating to the Isis cult have been found in many parts of the Roman world.

When the Roman Empire became Christian, the old religions of Egypt declined. Many temples were taken over to become monastic centres. Others had Christian churches built within them. Christian burial customs differed from the earlier ones in tending to include fewer grave goods with the burial. A few centres of the old Egyptian religion carried on. The Temple of Isis at Philae near Aswan continued the cult of Isis in Egypt until the reign of Justinian in the 6th century AD, and the closing of this temple may be considered to mark the end of the last phase in the practice of the religion of ancient Egypt.

TABLE OF EGYPTIAN RULERS

Many of the dates before the 27th Dynasty are approximate

EARLY DYNASTIC PERIOD 3100-2686

1ST DYNASTY 3100-2890
Narmer
Aha
Djer
Djet
Den
Queen Merneith
Anedjib
Semerkhet
Qaa

2ND DYNASTY 2890-2686
Hetepsekhemwy
Raneb
Nynetjer
Weneg
Sened
Peribsen
Khasekhemwy

OLD KINGDOM 2686-2181

3RD DYNASTY 2686-2613
Sanakht
Djoser (Zozer)
Sekhemkhet
Khaba
Huni

4TH DYNASTY 2613-2494
Sneferu	2613-2589
Khufu (Cheops)	2589-2566
Djedefre	2566-2558
Khafre (Chephren)	2558-2532
Menkaure (Mycerinus)	2532-2503
Shepseskaf	2503-2498

5TH DYNASTY 2494-2345
Userkaf	2494-2487
Sahure	2487-2475
Neferirkare	2475-2455
Shepseskare	2455-2448
Neferefre (Raneferef)	2448-2445
Nyuserre	2445-2421
Menkauhor	2421-2414
Djedkare	2414-2375
Unas	2375-2345

6TH DYNASTY 2345-2181
Teti	2345-2323
Userkare	2323-2321
Pepi I	2321-2287
Merenre	2287-2278
Pepi II	2278-2184
Nitiqret	2184-2181

FIRST INTERMEDIATE PERIOD 2181-2055

7TH AND 8TH DYNASTIES 2181-2124

9TH AND 10TH DYNASTIES 2160-2025
(Capital at Herakleopolis)
Meryibre (Khety)
Wahkare (Khety)
Merikare
Ity

11TH DYNASTY 2125-2055
(Capital at Thebes)
Mentuhotep I
Intef I	2125-2112
Intef II	2112-2063
Intef III	2063-2055

MIDDLE KINGDOM 2055-c.1700

11TH DYNASTY 2055-1985
Mentuhotep II	2055-2004
Mentuhotep III	2004-1992
Mentuhotep IV	1992-1985

12TH DYNASTY 1985-1795
Amenemhat I	1985-1955
Senusret I	1965-1920
Amenemhat II	1922-1878
Senusret II	1880-1874
Senusret III	1874-1855
Amenhemhat III	1855-1808
Amenhemhat IV	1808-1799
Queen Sobekneferu	1799-1795

13TH DYNASTY 1795-after 1650
Many rulers, including:
Hor
Khendjer
Sobekhotep III
Neferhotep I
Sobekhotep IV

14TH DYNASTY

SECOND INTERMEDIATE PERIOD c.1700-1550

15TH DYNASTY 1650-1550
Hyksos kings, ruling in the Delta
Salitis
Khyan
Apepi
Khamudi

16TH DYNASTY 1650-1550
Hyksos kings ruling in the Delta at the same time as the 15th Dynasty

17TH DYNASTY 1650-1550
Rulers at Thebes, including:
Intef
Taa I
Taa II
Kamose

NEW KINGDOM 1550-1069

18TH DYNASTY 1550-1295
Ahmose	1550-1525
Amenhotep I (Amenophis)	1525-1504
Thutmose I	1504-1492
Thutmose II	1492-1479
Thutmose III	1479-1425
Hatshepsut	1473-1458
Amenhotep II	1427-1400
Thutmose IV	1400-1390
Amenhotep III	1390-1352
Akhenaten (Amenhotep IV)	1352-1336
Smenkhkare	1338-1336
Tutankhamun	1336-1327

Ay	1327-1323
Horemheb	1323-1295

19TH DYNASTY 1295-1186

Rameses I	1295-1294
Seti I	1294-1279
Rameses II	1279-1213
Merenptah	1213-1203
Amenmessu	1203-1200
Seti II	1200-1194
Saptah	1194-1188
Tausret	1188-1186

20TH DYNASTY 1186-1069

Sethnakhte	1186-1184
Rameses III	1184-1153
Rameses IV	1153-1147
Rameses V	1147-1143
Rameses VI	1143-1136
Rameses VII	1136-1129
Rameses VIII	1129-1126
Rameses IX	1126-1108
Rameses X	1108-1099
Rameses XI	1099-1069

THIRD INTERMEDIATE PERIOD 1069-747

21ST DYNASTY 1069-945

(Capital at Tanis)

Smendes	1069-1043
Amenemnisu	1043-1039
Psusennes I	1039-991
Amenope	993-984
Osorkon the elder	984-978
Siamun	978-959
Psusennes II	959-945

Priest-kings at Thebes contemporary with Tanite Dynasty above:
Herihor
Paiankh
Pinudjem I
Masaherta
Menkheppere
Pinudjem II

22ND DYNASTY 945-715

(Capital at Bubastis)

Sheshonq I	945-924
Osorkon I	924-889
Sheshonq II	c. 890

Takelot I	889-874
Osorkon II	874-850
Takelot II	850-825
Sheshonq III	825-773
Pimay	773-767
Sheshonq V	767-730
Osorkon IV	730-715

23RD DYNASTY 818-715

Various ruling groups centred on Heracleopolis, Hermopolis, Tanis etc.

24TH DYNASTY 727-715

LATE PERIOD 747-332

25TH DYNASTY (KUSHITE)

(Capital at Thebes)

Piy	747-716
Shabaqo	716-702
Shabitqo	702-690
Taharqo	690-664
Tanutamani	664-656

26TH DYNASTY 664-525

(Capital at Sais)

Psamtek I	
	664-610
Nekay II	
	610-595
Psamtek II	
	595-589
Apries	
	589-570
Ahmose II	
	570-526
Psamtek III	526-525

27TH DYNASTY (PERSIAN RULE) 525-404

Cambyses	525-522
Darius I	522-486
Xerxes I	486-465
Artaxerxes I	465-424
Darius II	424-405
Artaxerxes II	405-359

28TH DYNASTY 404-399

(Capital at Sais)

Amyrtaios	404-399

29TH DYNASTY 399-380

(Capital at Mendes)

Nepherites I	399-393

Hakor	393-380
Nepherites II	c. 380

30TH DYNASTY 380-343

Nectanebo I	380-362
Teos	362-360
Nectanebo II	360-343

PERSIAN RULERS

343-332

Artaxerxes III	343-332
Arses	338-336
Darius III	336-332

MACEDONIAN AND PTOLEMAIC PERIOD 332-32

MACEDONIAN DYNASTY 332-305

Alexander the Great	332-323
Philip Arrhidaeus	323-317
Alexander IV	317-310

PTOLEMAIC DYNASTY

Ptolemy I Soter I	305-285
Ptolemy II Philadelphus	285-246
Ptolemy III Euergetes I	246-221
Ptolemy IV Philopator	221-205
Ptolemy V Epiphanes	205-180
Ptolemy VI Philometor	180-145
Ptolemy VII Neos Philometor	145
Ptolemy VIII Euergetes II	170-116
Ptolemy IX Soter II	116-107
Ptolemy X Alexander I	107-88
Ptolemy IX Soter II (restored)	88-80
Ptolemy XI Alexander II	80
Ptolemy XII Neos Dionysos	80-51
Cleopatra VII Philopator	51-30
Ptolemy XIII	51-47
Ptolemy XIV	47-44
Ptolemy XV Caesarion	44-30

ROMAN AND BYZANTINE PERIOD 30 BC-AD 642

Ruled by the Roman and Byzantine Emperors from 30 BC until the Arab conquest in AD 639-642.

INDEX

INDEX

INDEX